ID0604221

INTIMACY AND INFIDELITY

INTIMACY AND INFIDELITY
Separation-Individuation
Perspectives

edited by
Salman Akhtar, M.D.
and **Selma Kramer**, M.D.

JASON ARONSON INC.
Northvale, New Jersey
London

This book was set in 12 point Bem by TechType of Upper Saddle River, New Jersey, and printed and bound by Book-mart Press of North Bergen, New Jersey.

Library of Congress Cataloging-in-Publication Data

Intimacy and infidelity : separation-individuation perspectives /
    edited by Salman Akhtar and Selma Kramer.
        p.   cm.
    "Originally presented as papers at the 26th Annual Margaret S.
Mahler Symposium on Child Development held on May 6, 1995, in
Philadelphia"—Acknowledgment.
    Includes bibliographical references and index.
    ISBN 1-56821-775-7 (alk. paper)
    1. Intimacy (Psychology)   2. Separation-individuation.   3. Object
constancy (Psychoanalysis)   4. Object relations (Psychoanalysis)
5. Adultery.   I. Aktar, Salman, 1946 July 31–   II. Kramer, Selma.
III. Margaret S. Mahler Symposium on Child Development (26th : 1995
: Philadelphia, Pa.)
    [DNLM: 1. Interpersonal Relations—congresses.   2. Family—
psychology—congresses.   3. Extramarital Relations—congresses.
4. Sex Behavior—congresses.   5. Individuation—congresses.   WS
105.5.F2 I62 1996]
BF575.I5I573   1996
158'.2—dc20   96-4644

Manufactured in the United States of America. Jason Aronson Inc. offers books and cassettes. For information and catalog write to Jason Aronson Inc., 230 Livingston Street, Northvale, New Jersey 07647.

To the memory

of

Margaret S. Mahler,

teacher, friend, source of inspiration.

Contents

Contributors

Salman Akhtar, M.D.
Professor of Psychiatry, Jefferson Medical College; Training and Supervising Analyst, Philadelphia Psychoanalytic Institute, Philadelphia, Pennsylvania.

Lawrence D. Blum, M.D.
Director, Psychotherapy Training Program of the Philadelphia Psychoanalytic Institute and Society; Attending Psychiatrist, Institute of Pennsylvania Hospital, Philadelphia, Pennsylvania.

Alvin Frank, M.D.
Professor of Clinical Psychiatry, St. Louis University; Training and Supervising Analyst, St. Louis Psychoanalytic Institute, St. Louis, Missouri.

Louise J. Kaplan, Ph.D.
Co-editor of *The American Imago*; Member of the Professional
Advisory Board of the Margaret S. Mahler Research Founda-
tion; private practice of psychoanalysis, New York.

Selma Kramer, M.D.
Professor of Psychiatry, Jefferson Medical College; Training
and Supervising Analyst, Philadelphia Psychoanalytic Institute, Philadelphia, Pennsylvania.

Eric Lager, M.D.
Clinical Professor of Psychiatry, Hahnemann University
Hospital; Training and Supervising Analyst, Philadelphia
Psychoanalytic Institute, Philadelphia, Pennsylvania.

Helen C. Meyers, M.D.
Clinical Professor of Psychiatry, College of Physicians and
Surgeons, Columbia University; Training and Supervising
Analyst, Columbia University Center for Psychoanalytic
Training and Research, New York.

John M. Ross, Ph.D.
Clinical Professor of Psychiatry, Cornell University Medical
Center; Training and Supervising Analyst, Columbia Uni-
versity Center for Psychoanalytic Training and Research,
New York.

Acknowledgment

The chapters in this book, except the last one, were originally presented as papers at the 26th Annual Margaret S. Mahler Symposium on Child Development held on May 6, 1995, in Philadelphia. First and foremost, therefore, we wish to express our gratitude to the Margaret S. Mahler Psychiatric Research Foundation. We are also grateful to Troy L. Thompson II, M.D., Chairman, Department of Psychiatry and Human Behavior, Jefferson Medical College, as well as to the Philadelphia Psychoanalytic Institute and Society for their shared sponsorship of the symposium. Many colleagues from the Institute and Society helped during the symposium, and we remain grateful to them. Finally, we wish to acknowledge our sincere appreciation of Maryann Nevin for her efficient organization and assistance during the symposium and outstanding skills in the preparation of this book's manuscript.

1

THE DEVELOPMENT OF INTIMACY AND ITS RELATIONSHIP WITH THE ABILITY TO HAVE FRIENDS

Selma Kramer, M.D.

The ability to attain intimacy has many determinants. These include the individual's genetic endowment; the early mother–child interaction, including the status of the mother's mental health (which permits her to be close with her child as well as to relinquish her "possession" of him); the role of the father in the child's life, especially when he acts to interrupt the undue closeness of the child and the mother; childhood accidents and illnesses, as well as serious illness or death of significant people in the child's life; and, finally, the various friendships that the individual develops during his journey from childhood to adulthood.

In this chapter I focus on this last aspect of the capacity for intimacy. I trace roots of the ability to have friends within the symbiosis–separation–individuation process and the oedipal stage of development, through latency and adolescence, to the eventually mature emotional and sexual intimacy of adulthood. While I do focus mainly on the child's relationship with the mother, the role of the father (Abelin 1971,

Greenacre 1966, Loewald 1951, Mahler 1966) should in no way be underestimated.

THE DEVELOPMENTAL SUBSTRATE
OF INTIMACY

Intimacy is possible in the adult when the individual has achieved sufficient self-constancy (Mahler et al. 1975), has had experience with peer groups in latency and adolescence, and is no longer threatened by diffusion of ego boundaries and loss of the sense of self during sexual intercourse (Kernberg 1995), or by an extremely close emotional or intellectual relationship with a friend. Precursors of such intimacy arise as early as the symbiotic phase of development, when the mother–child relationship provides the child with the first experience of "we-ness" (Bergman 1980). This undifferentiated "we" experience forms the basis for later, more differentiated "we" experiences of true mutuality. Moreover, the symbiotic phase provides the child with healthy narcissism and trust in the outside world for gratification of basic needs. The first object of the outside world is the mother, of course; the ability to trust her is followed by a growth of "basic trust" (Erikson 1950) in others.

In the differentiation subphase, the child exerts a rudimentary push to grow away from the symbiotic closeness with the mother. He no longer molds to her body. Instead, he sits on her lap or at her feet, facing the outside world. During this period, it is normal, even imperative, for a child to react to persons other than the mother with anxiety. This affective reaction does not usually occur in response to the child's father, siblings, or other nonthreatening children. However, when a child displays no anxiety in response to adult strangers but instead goes to anyone, it suggests that his relationship with his mother is overly shallow. The associated "promiscuity" in accepting the overtures of strangers bodes ill for the possibility of developing deep and sustained object relationships.

In the joyous practicing subphase the child takes his first steps—usually *away* from his mother, a prelude to his walking and running with abandon. He explores his little world until he becomes aware that he has moved away from his mother. Now he runs back to her for "emotional refueling" (Furer, quoted in Mahler et al. 1975, p. 69). The emotional tone of this subphase is one of exhilaration. However, this exhilaration cannot last, because the toddler's physical ability to venture away from his mother, together with other concurrent maturational and cognitive strides, make him all too aware that his mother is not automatically at hand. At this time there is a great investment in sharing with her whatever he discovers in his roaming; at times he shadows her, but at the same time he is increasingly possessive and uses the words "me," "mine," and all too frequently "no!" This is the rapprochement subphase of separation-individuation. It is overlapped by the drive-based pressures of the late anal and beginning phallic-oedipal phases of development.

By the time the child reaches what Mahler called "on the way to self and object constancy" (Mahler 1966, Mahler and Furer 1968, Mahler et al. 1975), he shows increasing comfort when he is in one room while his mother is in another; often he prefers it. The child can now indulge in fantasy enactments and role playing. He can defer gratification, thus showing that basic trust has been formally established. Fusion of the good and bad object representations and good and bad self representations strengthens his ability to cope with simultaneous love and anger toward self and others (Kernberg 1975, Mahler and Furer 1968). The child's increasing reliance on verbalizing his needs and wishes, and his growing ability to spend pleasant time with an other-than-mother person, shows that the separation-individuation process is nearing completion. The parents, too, especially the mother, have to be comfortable "letting go" of the child for him to arrive at this developmental milestone.[1]

By age 3, the average child can attend nursery school, indicating that he is able to accept a mother substitute. His confidence in the internalized mother makes it possible for him to feel minimal intimacy with his teacher (almost invariably a woman!). The relationship with this teacher serves him well except when he is extremely tired or ill. Then only the mother can be of psychological benefit to him.

From 4 to 5 years of age, children show a need for friendships, even for having "best friends." This is the oedipal stage of development. During it there is a confluence of growth and development, of advance in psychosexual development and cognitive strides, and of the conflicting loving and hostile feelings toward both parents. The child has a healthy sense of himself as an individual and of his own sexual identity, though he continues to have strong residues of his earlier relationships with his parents. Object relations are strengthened by identification with the parent of the same sex and love of the parent of the opposite sex. Relationships with other children, at times, also get colored by these oedipal scenarios.

Case 1

Since birth David and Anita had spent a great deal of time together. Both sets of parents, longtime friends, worked, and

---

1. In less favorable circumstances, however, parents do not foster the child's individuation, for they may "need the child to be an extension of themselves because that is the only way they can understand the child" (Winnicott 1958, p. 93). In this context the observations of Mahler and Kaplan (1977) on children whose mothers had discouraged their locomotions and other autonomous functions are significant. These children show *stranger preference* in the place of "phase-specific stranger anxiety" (pp. 198–199).

although each had a reliable nanny, they familiarized each child with the parents, nanny, and home of the other in case one family was stuck without the nanny. When the children were 1½ to 2 years of age they were comfortable with each other, but engaged mostly in parallel play. By 3 they played with each other, spoke to each other, and were obviously drawn to each other. By 4 they were able to be intimate and imaginative. At age 4, David and Anita proclaimed that they loved each other and planned to get married. They even planned to have children! (This may have been stirred up by the fact that Anita's mother was pregnant.)

During latency, relationships with other-than-mother adults and with same-age peers broaden the child's psychosocial arena. The teacher may become a mother substitute, even one who may challenge the earlier omnipotence and omniscience of the mother in the child's mind. The assertion "My teacher told me so!" allows the child to question or even defy the mother's precepts and rules.

Case 2

Seven-year-old Amy told her mother that a fellow pupil, Pam, "could do the work if she really wants to but she doesn't try." Her mother had realized that Pam was intellectually retarded and told Amy that Pam might not be able to do as well in school as Amy and some others. The child protested, "My teacher said she doesn't try." Her mother temporarily dropped her attempts to help Amy become more compassionate and understanding of Pam.

In latency, friendships with same-gender peers are increasingly important. Children need a group of friends, and often a best friend, whose identity may change with some frequency. Friendships denote acceptance of the child by his peers,[2] and these bonds allow him to accept others even if they are less than perfect. Friendships also offer the child an opportunity to visit other families and to compare friends' parents with his own.

Case 3

> While visiting a friend's home for the first time, 8-year-old Adam, who was in analysis for severe learning problems and slight depression, was shocked to realize that not all fathers answer the doorbell in the evening with a raised revolver in hand. This experience revealed a family secret, one he felt he must now know—that his father engaged in criminal behavior.

In addition to peer friendships, some children are lucky enough to have an adult relative or friend who can become "a second mother" who helps in healthy separation or provides maternal care when a mother cannot function as a "good enough" mother to her children.

Early latency games such as hide-and-seek and tag focus on separation and reunion. In midlatency important games involve rules and punishment for breaking rules (Glenn 1991). "Giant steps" and "Did you say 'may I'?" are among the games that deal with superego issues, but now with peers and in an atmosphere of fun. By late latency and early adolescence structured "thinking" games include checkers, chess, and extend to Dungeons and Dragons, which helps the players (usually boys) symbolically explore the mysteries of an underworld arena of sex and aggression and provides each

---

2. Early in my career I felt that some mothers focused excessively on their children's popularity. I soon recognized, however, that these mothers were actually providing me with important material. The ability to have friends is a sign of a child's security in himself and in his mother, which enables him to trust other-than-mother figures.

player the possibility to be in control by being the dungeon master.

Friendships in late latency and adolescence involve sharing sexual secrets and, at times, mutual sexual stimulation. Rangell (1963), in a strikingly comprehensive psychoanalytic paper on friendships, highlights the dynamic ebb and flow in such relationships.

> Introjected objects, which have previously been absorbed into internal psychic structures, are now, during these still formative stages, reprojected and extrojected onto external objects, from which supplies are then reobtained and reintrojected. Such external sources serve as appendages, readily available reservoirs, for narcissistic supplies into which one can dip as necessary, to help the continuing process of psychic structuralization. [p. 21]

In the form of crushes and hero worship, idealized fantasies of intimacy continue until late adolescence, when the capacity for mature intimacy appears. Blos's (1967) "second individuation process of adolescence" delineates the increasing intrapsychic separation of the adolescent from his parents as primary love objects and as ego–ideal and superego figures, replacing them with nonparental objects, especially friends. The Tysons (1990) emphasize that

> the adolescent turns to his peers because of his need for relationships to gratify drive derivatives, to relieve his sense of emptiness, and to support his self-esteem as he pushes . . . toward psychic independence. . . . The peer group supplies nonjudgmental support as the adolescent attempts to resolve inner conflicts related to early object ties . . . the adolescent is therefore freer to experiment with others and with his own self in new situations with an increasing sense of independence. [p. 114]

The ability to take pleasure in sustained intimate relationships and to marry should be the final step in the development
of intimacy. Although deeply intimate with one main object,
the young adult is still able to maintain friendships. However,
friends are no longer as important as before. The primary love
objects (the parents) are, ideally, still loved and respected, but
never in such a way as to displace the importance of the
current and truly reciprocal love object. Winnicott (1984)
emphasizes that psychological health

> includes the idea of tingling life and the magic of intimacy. All
> these things go together and add up to a sense of feeling real
> and of being, and of the experiences feeding back into the
> personal psychic reality, enriching it, and giving it scope. The
> consequence is that the healthy person's inner world is related
> to the outer or actual world and yet is personal and capable of
> an aliveness of its own. . . . each person has a polite or social-
> ized self, and also a personal private self that is not available
> except in intimacy. [pp. 31, 66]

DISTURBANCES IN THE CAPACITY
FOR INTIMACY

Two clinical cases will help to illustrate disturbances in the
capacity for intimacy. The first recounts a woman's marital
infidelity, the second a man's more generalized impairments
in the realm of intimacy.

Case 4

> Jane was an attractive, well-coiffed married woman in
> her late thirties who came to treatment for severe PMS, mild
> depression, and a "constant fear that my parents may die
> young." She did not work, and felt that she was "only a
> housewife." Her husband was a busy accountant, so busy that

from December to mid-April he was almost totally unavailable to her and to their children.

Jane described her childhood as drab. She was the third daughter of a lower-middle-class family. She remembered her mother as an angry, strict woman, careful with the family's money, most of which she earned. Jane's mother appeared to be equally economical in doling out affection. Each day when she returned from work, she rested for an hour or two, unwilling to listen to her children, who were eager to tell her the events of the day. Yet Jane felt close to her mother and strangely safe with her. Jane's father had the task of cooking, caring for the children, and preparing them for bed. He was a "fun man," popular with friends, witty, and warm, but unsuccessful in business. Jane's mother criticized him for his careless manner of dressing, and it was obvious to Jane that her mother felt that she had married beneath herself.

Jane's sisters appeared to have been mother surrogates. She clung to them because in doing so she did not have to separate from her mother in an age-appropriate way. Jane explained that she had few friends because her sisters' friends were always around and it was so easy to be part of their groups. She did well in school, but when a high-school advisor offered to pursue a scholarship for her, Jane turned it down. She later realized that she feared becoming too educated, feeling superior to her family, and being resented for this. So she attended a two-year program leading to an associate degree in office management. She did well in her field and was assistant to the CEO of a flourishing business when she married.

In childhood and adolescence Jane was aware of the inequality between her parents' incomes and their positions in the family. She herself had vowed to marry a man who was a better provider, more serious, more hardworking than her father, and, indeed, she did. She married a successful CPA who was methodical and reliable but unexciting. She knew he loved her, but he was never demonstrative in public. Nor was he very imaginative in their erotic life. He did not try new sexual techniques and always left their bed immediately after sex to wash up, "as if I, or this entire sex act, were dirty." Jane said one day, "It's as though I had married my mother!" For a brief time she had dreams and fantasies about being sexually stimulated when she was cuddled by her mother. But she denied that these fantasies had any significance at all. She could recall that when she was very young, she would cling to her mother whenever possible. She remembered family walks in which her father walked ahead with an older sister on each arm, while she and her mother lagged behind. Jane felt secure and not jealous in such instances.

In the course of treatment, Jane soon "confessed" that she was having an affair with a carpenter who was working on an addition to their home. He was a good-looking, charming, debonair, and seductive Hispanic man. At times he was sweaty and emanated a body odor, but she did not find this unpleasant. She interjected with "My father never smelled, even though my mother said he was untidy." With the carpenter, sex was free and exciting. She did not worry that he might find her "dirty" when she initiated sex or suggested sexual variations her husband found perverse. Later on in treatment, Jane revealed that her inability to be sexually free with her husband originated not only from her husband's intolerance but also from her own inhibitions. These had arisen in the relationship with her mother, who had from early on disapproved of Jane's masturbation and sexual exploration. Her mother's seeing Jane as an extension of herself also precluded Jane's comfortable "ownership" of her own body and its sensations.

From the evolving clinical material in the subsequent months of treatment, it appeared that Jane was fixated at the preoedipal developmental stage of rapprochement and had not achieved self and object constancy. She had not achieved fusion of the "good" and "bad" mother, the "good" and "bad" father, or the "good" and "bad" self. She maintained compartmentalized views of them and of herself. Her bad mother was penny-pinching, critical of Jane's sexuality, and cold; the good mother was a source of security, safety, and some comfort (though she could not allow Jane to be appropriately on her own). The two representations of the mother were not combined, nor was the good, funny, exciting, and kind father combined with the bad, sexy, and dirty father. Jane viewed herself in similar terms. She was good in her marriage to a not very exciting man and bad in her adulterous affair with the carpenter. She felt as if she had married her mother, and when this marriage became impossible to sustain, she embarked on the affair, the most significant aspect of which was that her lover did not make her feel dirty. However, I feel it important to note that Jane did not achieve true emotional intimacy with either husband or lover. From her husband she not only kept the affair secret but secluded her overall erotic excitement. From her lover she kept hidden many aspects of her social and intellectual life. She was not truly intimate with either of them.

Case 5

Mr. D., a 45-year-old businessman, sought help when his wife threatened to leave him to get away from his constant misanthropy. He told me that he felt financially insecure, worthless, and so preoccupied with his mortgaging business that he had no time for his wife and children. When he did have some free time, he preferred to read from his collection of antique books rather than talk to his family. Sex was fair. In prior relationships sex had been satisfactory until he and his woman partner became close. Then he was intermittently impotent, a sexual problem that existed in his present marriage.

Mr. D. was given to warding me off out of fear of what closeness would bring. He told me that he did not know why he had entered treatment. He didn't expect me to be any better than his previous therapists, but maybe I could help him. As treatment progressed, his fear of closeness and of disappointment surfaced repeatedly in the transference. Although neither my name nor my appearance suggested it, he speculated that I must be of Italian Catholic heritage, as his father had been. His mother was higher class, an Irish Catholic from a wealthy family who were generous contributors to Catholic charities. It was obvious to my patient that his mother's family looked down on his father's (his maternal grandmother snubbed his father's mother, commenting on the garlic aura in her house).

Mr. D.'s father was so busy trying to prove his worth to his mother and her family that he was seldom home. When he was at home, he criticized the patient, deriding him for "stupidity, clumsiness, and being a momma's boy." Mr. D. was, in fact, too close to his mother. He was not encouraged to befriend other children in his neighborhood and thus felt compelled to follow his mother around. His mother was overly close to her son, sleeping with him when his father went away, bathing with him until she became aware of his sexual excitement and masturbation when he was about 4 years old. He said, "Then her smile ended."

One morning after four years of treatment, Mr. D. spoke of a "memory or a dream." "My parents were entertaining and were laughing. I was alone in my room and was bored. I knew they didn't want me with them. So I took a little china bowl from my mother's bathroom and I put something in it— maybe lighter fluid. I lit it and it flared up. I was terrified." The next day, after mentioning that he had had another disturbing dream that he could not recollect, Mr. D. announced that he had overslept and had not shaved before coming for his appointment. His tone of voice was defiant, as if anticipating (and also intending to provoke) my criticism. As if I were prodding him to explain why he had not shaved, he said, "Once in a while I can't stand to look into the mirror. I don't know whom I'll see—my high-class Irish self or my low-class Italian self, or my accepting mother or rejecting mother." He associated to the "memory or dream" of the previous day. The noisy party could be primal scene (he added wryly that at least he had gotten this much out of his earlier treatment!). He could not associate to the fire until he suddenly said, "My father's aftershave! It made him smell good. I put some on my body and it burned. I guess I put it on my penis. There was no use in asking for help. My parents would have blamed and shamed me."

As an adolescent Mr. D. mutilated his face by picking his pimples until his skin bled. His mother looked at him with disgust. He couldn't look at himself in the mirror, for he would see his mother's sneer or his own mutilated face. He felt that his mother wanted him to be a source of pride with her family and friends and that he seldom fulfilled this need.

In high school and college he had few friends. After graduating from college, he felt that having friends would mean he was normal, but he often ruined friendships by looking down on the friends. He married because it was the proper thing to do. However, he could not get close to his wife and children. He was untrusting of them and remained somewhat aloof from them. He felt that his children were expensive toys for his wife's pleasure. He revealed that in an earthquake he would hastily gather up his antique books and an antique lamp. Only after he had put them in a safe place would he reenter his home to rescue his children. He then said to me, as if I had remonstrated, "I can't get intimate with anyone, not my wife, not my kids, not with you. Only books and lamps are safe. They don't disappoint me, and I don't disappoint them."

As the treatment progressed, we could see that Mr. D. had not attained self or object constancy. In fact, it appeared that his parents themselves had not evolved a sustained, loving view of one another; each harshly disliked the "bad qualities" of the other. Mr. D. felt that his normal, age-appropriate behavior represented to his mother the bad qualities of the Italian Catholics (sexy and dirty) and to his father a projection of a side of himself that was never acceptable. To the father he was, in part, an Irish Catholic who might look down on him, in part an Italian Catholic who was doomed to be a failure in the eyes of higher-class people. As a child Mr. D. often felt ignored by each parent (a nanny cared for him) and felt he was used as a pawn between them. In addition, he was used as an object of combined parental disappointment and contempt. He did not learn to trust his parents. Only in his paternal grandfather did he find empathy and reliability, but this grandfather was Italian and thus to Mr. D.'s mind, "contaminated."

It was obvious that he could not achieve intimacy and was emotionally isolated throughout his childhood, adolescence, and adulthood. When treatment permitted some intimacy with others, he was afraid to leave the safety of isolation, and undertook an adulterous relationship in which he could have "fun" without commitment.

CONCLUDING REMARKS

The relationship between the impaired capacity for intimacy and eventual infidelity in a marriage has drawn considerable psychoanalytic attention. For example, Eisenstein (1956) states, "Emotionally immature people are incapable of experiencing satisfactory interpersonal intimacy, including heterosexual activity" (p. 102). He says later, "Sexual frigidity very commonly results in marital infidelity—the frigid wife searches for sexual satisfaction; the husband reacts to his frigid and unresponsive wife" (p. 107). He goes on to comment that "marital infidelity on the part of either partner does not necessarily denote psychopathology. However, the more primitive the personality organization, the more infantile and impulsive the character formation, the more exaggerated will be the degree of 'acting out' as sexual promiscuity" (p. 108).

Among his many publications on aspects of the vicissitudes of love, sex, and marriage in the context of normality and pathological personality disorders, Kernberg (1995) has written a broadly encompassing treatise on the subject. He addresses differences between men and women in the capacity for tolerating discontinuities regarding love relations, and states that while women discontinue sexual relations with a man they no longer love, men usually can maintain a sexual relationship with a woman even if they no longer love the woman, but love someone else. He states (p. 84), "Men's discontinuity between erotic and tender attitudes toward women is reflected in the 'madonna–prostitute' dissociation."³ Kernberg further suggests that "one may say that men and women have to learn throughout time what the other comes prepared with in establishing a love relationship: for men, to achieve a commitment in depth, and for women, sexual freedom" (pp. 84–85).

Simon (1977) proposes that since women are allowed greater emotional expression than men, they have greater comfort and ease with intimacy. Many men find it easier to function well sexually without love or affection toward women, while a woman needs to care for a man to give herself sexually to him. Simon uses a developmental approach in saying that

> the concept for (adult) intimacy . . . rests on a secure sense of one's own self and one's own boundaries [for in such situations] sexual desire, orgastic fulfillment, and commitment to the other do not pose any threat of personal dissolution. . . . The identity of each becomes further consolidated and expanded through their intimacy, not fragmented or diminished. [p. 332]

Infidelity is created by an emotional anlage in which errors in development that repeated have not permitted intimacy and fidelity to be complete. I will conclude by mentioning a vignetted offered by a colleague for this chapter. He was asked to evaluate a young woman who complained of depression. In my colleague's report, he described the woman as being unable to achieve intimacy. The referring physician disagreed, saying that the patient's many affairs proved that she could, indeed, achieve intimacy! I agree with my colleague who was able to distinguish between promiscuity and intimacy. It is my hope that the various contributions to this volume will underscore this distinction while highlighting the origins and vicissitudes of both intimacy and infidelity.

---

3. This appeared in the case of Jane, who could not be sexually free with her husband (who resembled her mother) but could be free with a lower-class laborer (who resembled her father).

REFERENCES

Abelin, E. (1971). The role of the father in the separation-individuation process. In *Separation-Individuation*, ed. J. McDevitt and C. Settlage, pp. 229–252. New York: International Universities Press.

Bergman, A. (1980). Ours, yours, mine. In *Rapprochement: The Critical Subphase of Separation-Individuation*, ed. R. F. Lax, S. Bach, and J. A. Burland, pp. 199–216. New York: Jason Aronson.

Blos, P. (1967). The second individuation process of adolescence. *Psychoanalytic Study of the Child* 22:162–186. New York: International Universities Press.

Eisenstein, V. (1956). Sexual problems in marriage. In *Neurotic Interaction in Marriage*, pp. 101–124. New York: Basic Books.

Erikson, E. H. (1950). *Childhood and Society*. New York: W. W. Norton.

Glenn, J. (1991). Transformations in normal and pathological latency. In *Beyond the Symbiotic Orbit: Advances in Separation-Individuation Theory*, ed. S. Akhtar and H. Parens, pp. 171–188. Hillsdale, NJ: Analytic Press.

Greenacre, P. (1966). Problems of overidealization of the analyst and of analysis: their manifestations in the transference and countertransference relationships. *Psychoanalytic Study of the Child* 21:193–212. New York: International Universities Press.

Kernberg, O. F. (1975). *Borderline Conditions and Pathological Narcissism*. New York: Jason Aronson.

——— (1995). *Love Relations: Normality and Pathology*. New Haven, CT: Yale University Press.

Loewald, H. W. (1951). Ego and reality. *International Journal of Psycho-Analysis* 32:10–18.

Mahler, M. S. (1966). Discussion of Greenacre's paper "Problems of Overidealization of the Analyst and of Analysis: Their Manifestations in the Transference and Countertransference Relationships." *Psychoanalytic Quarterly* 36:637.

Mahler, M. S., and Furer, M. (1968). *On Human Symbiosis and the Vicissitudes of Individuation.* Vol. 1. *Infantile Psychosis*. New York: International Universities Press.

Mahler, M. S., and Kaplan, L. (1977). Developmental aspects in the assessment of narcissistic and so-called borderline personalities. In *The Selected Papers of Margaret S. Mahler*, vol. 2, ed. M. H. Harley and A. Weil, pp. 195–209. New York: Jason Aronson, 1979.

Mahler, M. S., Pine, F., and Bergman, A. (1975). *The Psychological Birth of the Human Infant*. New York: Basic Books.

Rangell, L. (1963). On friendship. *Journal of the American Psychoanalytic Association* 11:3–54.

Simon, B. (1977). Early adulthood. In *Understanding Behavior in Health and Illness*, ed. B. Simon and H. Pardes, pp. 324–335. Baltimore, MD: Williams and Wilkins.

Tyson, P., and Tyson, R. L. (1990). *Psychoanalytic Theories of Development*. New Haven: Yale University Press.

Winnicott, D. W. (1958). *Collected Papers*. New York: Basic Books.

——— (1984). *Home Is Where We Start From*. New York: W. W. Norton.

2

TRANSFORMATIONS OF NARCISSISM: FROM "OMNIPOTENTIALITY" TO FIDELITY

Louise J. Kaplan, Ph.D.

When Selma Kramer requested that I address the subject of fidelity, rather than intimacy or infidelity, I found myself pondering the possible relationships between *intimacy,* a personal psychological capacity, and *fidelity,* a social value or ideal. And the more I mused on the word *fidelity,* the more I kept coming back to Erik Erikson's (1964) "Human Strength and the Cycle of Generations." In that essay Erikson spoke of fidelity as the vital virtue, or ego strength, that emerges from the adolescent process, and he defined fidelity as "the ability to sustain loyalties freely pledged in spite of the contradictions of value systems" (p. 125).

After deciding that my chapter would concern issues pertaining to the moral life and adolescent development, I was still left with the dilemma of how to relate all this to Mahler's writings on separation-individuation. To be faithful to the spirit of Mahler's thought, I could not solve my dilemma by reducing later developmental outcomes to their infantile precursors. Furthermore, like me, Mahler deplored recapitula-

21

tionist versions of human development, particularly the popular notion that adolescence is a recapitulation of infantile separation-individuation.

My immediate dilemma turned out to be an inspiration for a chapter on the transformations of narcissism that play a crucial role in the regulation of the moral life—a central but frequently overlooked theme in the writings of Margaret Mahler. I realized that the aspects of Mahler's theory most germane to the topic of fidelity are her general formulations on narcissism and, specifically, her appreciation of the paradoxical relations between narcissism and aggression.

Erikson (1964) said that "trustworthy motherliness needs a trustworthy 'universe' " (p. 152), and he also made a plea for the intergenerational continuities (pp. 152–157) that facilitate the moral and ethical sensibilities of children and adolescents. Mahler seldom wrote directly about these sensibilities. However, in *The Psychological Birth of the Human Infant* (1975a), and in the several papers that I will discuss below, she delineated the transformations of narcissism that contribute to the internalizations and identifications that are intrinsic to the structuring of superego and ego ideal.

Before turning to Mahler's work, I will set the context by reviewing Erikson's thoughts on virtue; presenting a brief overview of the modern history of the tensions between family attachments and the moral and ethical structures that arise in connection with the preservation of civilization; and recalling Freud's pessimistic outlook on the capacity of family attachments to regulate and contain the aggressive drive. At that point I will bring in Mahler's writings on narcissism, emphasizing her distinctions between self-love and self-esteem, which are more closely allied with libidinal strivings and separation, and omnipotence, which is more closely allied with aggressive strivings and individuation.[1]

---

1. Readers will note that my distinctions between the separation and individuation strands of the separation-individuation process and those of Meyers (this volume) are not identical.

It is compatible with our intuitive sense of the emotional life to regard fidelity as a derivative of libidinal strivings and certain vicissitudes of self-love and self-esteem. However, I have chosen to explore some less obvious correlations between fidelity and transformations of omnipotence. In doing so, I am also suggesting that the emergence of fidelity in adolescence is related to some of the transformations of aggression that were discussed in the previous volume in this series dedicated to the memory of Mahler, *The Birth of Hatred* (Akhtar et al. 1995).

According to Erikson (1964), the negative of virtue is not vice but certain weaknesses of the ego that leave the person vulnerable to symptoms of "disorder, dysfunction, disintegration [and] anomie" (p. 139). The vital virtues emerge in a sequence that corresponds to the various stages of the life cycle. After acquiring the capacity for hope in earliest infancy, the child goes on to develop the ego strengths of will, purpose, and competence, in other words, the autonomy, initiative, and pride that give a child the sense that she is in control of her actions and destiny. Adolescence is the time for the emergence of fidelity, the capacity to pledge one's loyalty to ideals and social values. The virtues of care and wisdom emerge during the two stages of adulthood, enabling parents and grandparents to transmit the vital virtues to the next generation.

Our ethical sense, the cultural conscience that says we should care as deeply for the welfare of neighbors, colleagues, society, and so on—the human community—as for our own self-interest depends, to a certain extent, on the ego strengths described by Erikson. And, as he suggested (1964, p. 113), in the absence of the personal vigor, animation, and integrity of virtue, sublime moral aims collapse into puerile moralisms, and ethical ideals wither into feeble conformities to law and order.

On the other hand, as we all know, strenuous virtue all

too often verges on cruel exigency. The demands we place on ourselves and on others for moral excellence can sometimes lead to piety and self-righteousness and, alas, more often to acts of destructive aggression than to acts of altruism.

FROM ENLIGHTENMENT TO THE MODERN ANTIUTOPIAN VIEWS

In Western civilization during the Enlightenment, philosophers and poets began to appreciate that the child was not a miniature adult but a little being whose moral sense would not flourish unless his biological and psychological needs were met by the nurturance of a charitable and compassionate mothering person. Before too long a backlash turned the Enlightenment on its head. The so-called discovery of childhood was said to be one strand in the general web of deceit. Childhood and adolescence were said to be mere cultural contrivances having very little, if anything, to do with biological and psychological necessities. The bourgeois family was said to be designed so that children could effectively be indoctrinated into the marketplace economy with its virtues of hard work, strict gender categories, consumption, and leisure. The bonds of love were exposed as the mother's gentle seductions into the bondage of the workplace. The high cultural forms of the Enlightenment, the sciences, the letters, the arts, were invented to "spread garlands of flowers over the iron chains with which men are burdened . . . and make them love their slavery" (Rousseau [1755] 1964, p. 36). So declared Jean-Jacques Rousseau, the Enlightenment *philosophe* who paradoxically would be hailed as the inventor of the icons of the modern age, among them motherhood, childhood, and adolescence.

The most frequently cited contemporary text on the invention theory of childhood is Philippe Aries' (1960)

Centuries of Childhood. According to Aries, until the Enlightenment the child was free. Afterward, the solicitude of family and church would inflict on the carefree, bondless child "the birch, the prison cell—in a word, the punishments usually reserved for convicts from the lowest strata of society" (p. 413). Aries enlists *The Little Prince* as an ideal of childhood that would have appalled Saint Exupéry. True, Saint Exupéry said that his cosmic urchin from asteroid B-612 was

> free, infinitely free, so free that he was no longer conscious of pressing on the ground. He was free of that weight of human relationships which impedes movement, those tears, those farewells, those reproaches, those joys, all that a man caresses or tears as he sketches out a gesture, those countless bonds which tie him to others and make him heavy. [Aries 1969, p. 411]

But Saint Exupéry wrote these words as a lament to the suffering of his Little Prince. At the time, Saint Exupéry was living in exile in New York and suffering profoundly from the innumerable losses he had sustained after France had fallen to the Nazis. His Little Prince was a lost child who had flown away to an imaginary planet so that he would not be overwhelmed by his feelings of loss. The bonds that tied him to others had been torn asunder. So great were his pain and longing, the Little Prince could not weep. His re-descent to earth, his regaining of his sense of human community, his growing attachments to other living beings enable the Little Prince to experience all that he has lost and at last to weep. In Aries' lopsided interpretation of Saint Exupéry's words, a child who is not bound by human attachments is gloriously free.

Impervious to criticisms of his theories of childhood, Aries continued to promulgate the notion that human beings were better off in those centuries when attachments were

"diffuse, spread out equally over numerous natural and super-
natural objects including God, saints, parents, children,
friends, horses, dogs or orchards and gardens" (1977, p. 229).

Children do sometimes suffer deeply from the intensities
of family passion. And surely the increasing isolation and
privatization of the family that Aries describes exacerbated the
mental torments from which all family members would suffer. However, we must suspect the totalitarian impulses underlying Aries' claim that the sufferings of childhood would
be alleviated by diluting the passions of family life. The
alacrity with which Aries and other twentieth-century social
philosophers blame the bourgeois family for all our ills suggests that the family is being used as a scapegoat for other
social institutions whose culpabilities they prefer not to identify or scrutinize.

Before the Enlightenment princes would argue convinc-
ingly that their ethic of slavery and domination was designed
for the general good. Initially, the democratic, entrepreneurial
spirit of the Industrial Revolution was a major force in ener-
gizing the Enlightenment mentality that would eventually
eliminate the princedoms and aristocracies that Aries idealizes.
Nevertheless, soon the princes of industry began to emulate
the ethical mannerisms of the princes of yore. In the guise of a
business ethics intended for the general good, modern business morality maneuvers any number of appeals to reason and
rationality for its flagrant duplicities and ruthless vandalisms.
Sentient human beings, however, need a different order of
ethics. To survive the plight of being human, we require an
ethics of passion and desire, if you will, a consensus of com-
passion and fidelity.

Even as Aries was singing the virtues of medieval society
and advancing his fanciful visions of childhood freedom, these
virtues and visions had already, once again, become actualities. As the twentieth century advanced and public opinion,
general consensus, and pragmatic morality replaced the stren-

uous vigilance of conscience, Aries' unattached prince, armed with every grandiosity and vanity of his wondrous narcissistic aloofness, took up residence as the ruler and ruling spirit of the bourgeois family. The child and adolescent in whom the latter-day child-centered family had invested so much value would now carry the combined burden of a wavering conscience and a sense of omnipotence and grandiose self-entitlement. The family cocoon that was supposed to have sheltered the individual against the indignities of the industrial machine age disintegrated into a temporary, ramshackle campsite, an accommodation to expediency, just barely held together by the vagrant passions of its adult members. Aries' prince, unfettered by any ties of affection or love, was the vanguard and standard-bearer of the "me" generation, a free-for-all quest for personal liberation in which each family member, including the child, was on his or her own in the pursuit of self-fulfillment and freedom. As Christopher Lasch (1977) observed in *Haven in a Heartless World,* the family more and more came to resemble the harsh world outside. "Relations within the family took on the same character as relations elsewhere; individualism and the pursuit of self-interest reigned even in the most intimate of institutions" (p. 35).

Potentially, at least, parents provide children with the leniency and charity that might mitigate the calculated indifference of the business morality that pervades the larger social order. As the social institution assigned to mediate between the crude, unformed nature of the child and society, the family must promote the impersonalized values of civilization even as the family simultaneously (sometimes surreptitiously) encourages the cherishing of children by parents, emotional intimacy among its members, and the maintenance of intergenerational continuities. Thus, the family is always at once the transmitter of civilization and the transmitter of those personal passions that engender a healthy antagonism to the "business as usual" interests of society.

Paradoxically, therefore, the very bonds of affection and love between parent and child are often regarded as a threat to the structures of society.

Utopias, actual and imaginary, eradicate the resistance to community by eradicating the family. In Plato's *Republic,* Thomas More's *Utopia,* Rousseau's *Emile,* Thoreau's *Walden,* B. F. Skinner's *Walden Two,* the first order of business in establishing a utopian society was to separate the child from the family. In the so-called antiutopian literature, such as Huxley's *Brave New World,* Zamyatin's *We,* George Orwell's *1984,* the utopian practice of removing the child from the family is exposed as the first step in a totalitarian regime of constant surveillance, of regulated sexuality, of suppressed individuality, of banished poets, of outlawed memory and desire. And as these antiutopian authors forcefully remind us, there is certainly no place for adolescent rebellion in Utopia.

FREUD'S PESSIMISM REGARDING THE CONTAINMENT OF HUMAN AGGRESSION

Shortly after World War I, and barely one year after Freud published the German edition of *Beyond the Pleasure Principle,* the British psychoanalyst J. C. Flugel (1921) asserted that

> all schemes and attempts that have been made, from Plato onwards (and probably long before him), with a view to preventing the development of the feelings that centre in and are aroused through connection with the family are doomed to failure:—practical failure, because these feelings are too strong, too intimate and essential a part of human nature to be successfully and permanently inhibited by alteration of the environment; moral failure because the development of certain of the most important aspects of human character are, in their origin and first appearance, bound up with family feel-

ings and would probably fail to ripen if these feelings were abolished. [p. 140]

In *Beyond the Pleasure Principle* Freud (1920) was not optimistic about the power of family attachments to resist their own destruction. When Freud considered the wanton cruelty and violence of a war conducted in the name of justice, he wondered if there was any hope at all for the survival of the human species. The war demonstrated, on a communal level, a destructive force that Freud had long suspected in his individual patients. Beyond the urgencies for pleasure and self-preservation that inspired psychological growth and moral progression was another force that undermined the unity of the human soul. Thanatos, the death instinct, must be more powerful than Eros, the instinct that unites one human being with another and carries the species forward toward increasingly higher moral and ethical unities.

Freud acknowledged the speculative nature of his thoughts on the death instinct, saying that he had thrown himself into this pessimistic line of thought in order to challenge psychoanalysis with questions it could not yet answer (pp. 58–61). Freud confessed to being the devil's advocate (p. 59) and also confessed that he would like very much, given the chance, to argue for the other side (pp. 59–61). He concluded by taking comfort in the slow advances of psychoanalytic knowledge. "What we cannot reach flying we must reach limping. . . . The Book tells us it is no sin to limp" (p. 64).

Ten years later, in *Civilization and Its Discontents,* Freud returned to do battle with the devil. The psychoanalytic advances of the decade between 1920 and 1930 had put Freud in a better position to argue for Eros. Previously, the great debate between desire and authority was posed as a power struggle—as if sexuality and conscience were at war; as if there were only two parties in the dispute; as if conscience alone could defend civilization against the polymorphous mayhem of human sexuality; as if the survival of civilization depended on the renunciation, suppression, and extinction of desire.

With the advent of Freud's ego psychology[2] in the mid-1920s, there would be three agencies of mind—id, ego, and superego. Instead of two warring parties, there would be three protagonists. The ego, though less powerful in brute force than either id or superego, is more ingenious. The ego can apprehend the demands of reality and transmit these demands to id and superego in a way that makes them tolerable. As the agency of mind that engages external reality, the ego can also effect the satisfactions of id and superego. The ego can negotiate compromises wherein id impulses are given expression in a form that also mollifies the superego. However, when it comes to modifications and transformations of aggression, the ego pays an awesome price for its ingenuities.

By internalizing the destructive aggressions that might be vented on the world and transforming them into aspects of conscience, the ego replaces the violence of external authority with an internal virulence that undermines its own integrity. "A threatened external unhappiness—loss of love and punishment on the part of the external authority—has been exchanged for a permanent internal unhappiness, for the tension of the sense of guilt" (1930, p. 128). Would the survival of the species depend, then, on an increasing severity of conscience? If the only inducements to care as much for the preservation of the species as we care for our own self-preservation are the intimidations of guilt, then perhaps the critics who survey "the aims of cultural endeavour and the means it employs" (p. 144) might be correct in their pessimistic conclusion that "the whole effort is not worth the trouble, and that the outcome of

---

2. For the convenience of narrative style I speak of id, ego, and superego as if they were tangible entities. However, id, ego, and superego are aspects or constituents or agencies of mind (itself not a tangible entity) and not to be confused with tangible persons, places, or things, or even tangible forces.

it can only be a state of affairs which the individual will be unable to tolerate" (p. 145).

Nevertheless, there was some hope. If the ego's ingenuities of modification, compromise, negotiation, and transformation could collaborate with Eros in transforming self-interest into an interest in preserving the species, perhaps Thanatos could be kept at bay.

Originally, Freud spoke of narcissism as antagonistic to attachment and concern for others. Now that he had a clearer vision of how, in the course of development, the ego modified crude excitement into erotic longings for others, he considered the possibility that narcissism might be transformed into a motive and inspiration for altruism.

Freud never solved the problem of how human beings were to achieve this crucial transformation of narcissism. And psychoanalysis is still limping along with the rest of the world in trying to arrive at a solution. However, as early as 1905, Freud suggested when, and even how, this transformation might take place. At puberty, the family must surrender the child to society. At puberty, the child must relinquish her infantile ties to her parents so that she may go on to establish her own family, her own version of commitment or noncommitment to the values of the larger social order. At puberty, the friendly relations between family life and civilization become highly equivocal. Out of this ubiquitous intergenerational tension and the conflicts that it stirs up emerges a new transformation of narcissism and with it a potential for fidelity.

MAHLER'S PERSPECTIVE ON THE TRANSFORMATIONS OF NARCISSISM

Though Mahler did not address the issue of adolescent moral and ethical commitment, her writings consistently testify to the fact that different qualities of object relations arise in conjunction with specific transformations of narcissism.

From the beginning, even as Mahler was writing almost exclusively on childhood psychosis and various other forms of deviant and pathological development, one of her major themes concerned transformations of narcissism. For example, in her 1959 paper "On Infantile Precursors of the 'Influencing Machine' (Tausk)" written in collaboration with Paula Elkisch, Mahler described how the transformation of primary narcissism into secondary narcissism was dependent on the progressive libidinization of the infant's body surface by the mother. By deflecting aggression away from the inside of the body, this fundamental transformation enabled the development of secondary narcissistic cathexes to the central and peripheral parts of the body that Mahler suggested were "prerequisites for the partial introjective and projective mechanisms which lead via normal identification to separation from the mother" (p. 206). Moreover, in this essay written several years before the precise details of the separation-individuation process had been worked out, Mahler's understanding of the transformations from primary to secondary narcissism was enabling her to delineate the differences between the separation and individuation strands. She said:

> It seems that contact-perceptual and kinesthetic experiences are essential for the development of the body image in its central and peripheral parts (Greenacre, 1953) as well as for the formation of the self (Jacobson, 1954), whereas distance perceptions seem to facilitate separation from the mother's body and demarcation of the own body image from the environment. [p. 206]

Mahler goes on to state that the formation of the ego "is dependent on both of these processes—upon the contact- and distance-perceptual experiences" (p. 206). Thus, as early as

1959 Mahler was implying that the ego evolves in conjunction with the transformations of narcissism that are intrinsic to separation-individuation.

In that same early paper Mahler demonstrated how an overstimulation of contact experiences with a frustration of distance experiences leads to "a symbiotic parasitism" (p. 208) necessitating a total introjection of the mother to ward off separation panic. "When the mother is totally introjected, this very mechanism removes her as the beacon of reality orientation to the real world" (p. 208). In other words, if there is a developmental interference with the requisite transformations from primary to secondary narcissism, the mother cannot be cathected with secondary narcissism or attain the status of an independent object.

Two years later, in "On Sadness and Grief in Infancy and Childhood," Mahler (1961) reiterated this idea. "Only when the body becomes the object of the infant's secondary narcissism, via the mother's loving care, does the external object become available for identification" (p. 264). She alluded briefly to the relationship between narcissism and "the vicissitudes of the aggressive drive" (p. 264) and in that connection spoke of the dramatic narcissistic transformations that were intrinsic to the (as yet unnamed) practicing phase of separation-individuation.

> The toddler is able to experiment with, practice and enjoy the autonomous functions of his ego only if personality development and maturation proceed at a comparable rate. Mastery of these functions gives the child secondary narcissistic pleasure, as Hendrick (1942) has pointed out. Moreover, such experiences eventually help the child to acquire a sense of individual identity. [p. 264]

After having learned more about the effects of autonomous ego functioning on the toddler's narcissistic equilibrium, Mahler returned to this theme of the complex relationship between the development of affects and transformations of narcissism. In "Notes on the Development of Basic Moods: The Depressive Affect," Mahler (1966) distinguishes the narcissism of the differentiation phase from that of the practicing phase. Whereas during the differentiation subphase the infant shows a heightened vitality and sustained interactions with the world of reality when close to the mother, in a few months the narcissistic balance shifts. During practicing, narcissism is at its height and elation is the basic mood (pp. 66–67). The child's narcissistic investment in her own functions as well as in the objects and objectives of reality takes precedence over concerns about the mother's whereabouts. However, if the child is to achieve a genuine independence from the mother and genuine autonomy, the ideal state of self achieved during practicing must be divested of its delusional aspects.

Gradually, the sense of mastery leads to a heightened awareness of separateness and the ensuing rapprochement crisis, with its potential for an "acute deflation of the child's omnipotence and a serious injury to his narcissism" (p. 67).

As Mahler states:

The two pillars of early infantile well-being and self-esteem are the child's belief in his own omnipotence and his belief in the parents' omnipotence, of which he partakes; these beliefs can be replaced only gradually by a realistic recognition of, belief in, and enjoyment of his individual autonomy, and by the development of object constancy. [p. 70]

The next year, 1967, Mahler published "On Human Symbiosis and the Vicissitudes of Individuation," in which she describes how the senior toddler's growing autonomy begins to correct his delusional estimation of his own omnipotence. This corrective to his own narcissism allows for a greater degree of internalization of the parents' demands and the beginnings of "true ego identification with the parents" (p. 90). However, as the observations of the toddler, Jay, demonstrate, when the delusional aspects of the child's omnipotence cannot be modified, individuation propelled by innate maturational forces usually proceeds but separation is hampered, a psychological situation that engenders serious discrepancies in the child's lines of development. And as Mahler (1971) later pointed out in "A Study of the Separation-Individuation Process and Its Possible Applications to Borderline Phenomena in the Clinical Situation," these narcissistic imbalances lead to serious deficits in the integrative and synthetic functions of the ego, among them deficits in superego–ego ideal structures (p. 181).

In one of her last published papers, "On the Current Status of the Infantile Neurosis," Mahler (and colleagues 1975b) highlighted the dynamic interplay between narcissism, object relations, and the infantile neurosis (p. 189). She described the convergence of the three paramount anxieties of childhood during rapprochement—fear of object loss, fear of losing the object's love, and premature precipitation of castration anxiety and penis envy (p. 192). She referred to the pervasive separation anxiety of patients whose affects are dominated by narcissistic rage (p. 193).

Mahler found confirmation for her evolving theory of narcissistic transformation in Spruiell's 1975 paper "Three Strands of Narcissism." Spruiell consented to the popular idea that "the clinical and theoretical understanding of narcissism would open new territories for psychoanalysis"; he also cautioned that "the topic continues to be bedeviled by ambiguities, misunderstandings and unnecessary metapsychological constructs" (p. 577).

After pointing to various definitions of narcissism as a phase, a perversion, a method of regulating self-esteem, an aspect of self-love, a type of object choice; as omnipotence;

and in terms of secondary structures like the ego-ideal aspect of the superego, Spruiell proposed that three of these forms—self-love, the regulations of self-esteem, and omnipotence—be treated as separate, related variables, or perhaps independent lines of development, "which may become integrated and mingled in the healthy individual but which may be kept apart pathologically, or individually stunted, or compensatorily intensified, swollen and overused" (p. 579).

Spruiell follows the pattern, suggested in Pumpian-Mindlin's 1969 "Vicissitudes of Infantile Omnipotence," of differentiating omnipotence from the other two forms of narcissism. Whereas self-esteem and self-love are predominantly derivatives of libido, omnipotence (insofar as it is related to issues of action and power) is predominantly a derivative of aggression—"especially if aggression is thought of as consisting of more than simply destruction" (p. 582). To amplify this particular aspect of his more general thesis, Spruiell referred to Mahler's observations on the "flowering of omnipotence in the first half of the second year as the toddler creates a marvelous world almost totally experienced as being within his control" (p. 583). He then spoke of adult patients whose complexly determined pathology included "specific narcissistic aggressive problems traceable to interference with, or unusual augmentation of, this 'flowering of omnipotence' " (p. 583).

Mahler's most advanced perspectives on the transformations of narcissism and their impact on the formation of the superego were informed by Spruiell's paper. In our collaborative essay "Developmental Aspects in the Assessment of Narcissistic and So-Called Borderline Personalities" (1977), Mahler begins by linking the fourth organizer, the Oedipus complex, to specific transformations of narcissism afforded by each phase of separation-individuation (p. 195).

With Spruiell's distinctions between self-love, self-esteem, and omnipotence in mind, she notes how 5- to 8-

month-old infants, "surrounded by approving and libidinally mirroring friendly adults, seemed electrified and stimulated by this reflecting admiration" (p. 197). She describes how during the symbiotic phase as well as in the differentiation and early practicing subphases narcissism is dependent on fueling by the environment. Mahler's formulations suggest that self-love and self-esteem are dependent on object relations, whereas omnipotence is related to aggressive strivings and fueled from within.

> The *autonomous achievements* of the practicing subphase are the main source of narcissistic enhancement from *within*. Most infant-toddlers of the practicing stage show three contributories to narcissism at their peak. These are (in an exaggerated way and in individually different proportions): self-love, primitive valuations of their accomplishments and omnipotence. During the rapprochement subphase, prior to and dependent on the resolutions of the rapprochement crisis, narcissism (particularly omnipotence shaken by the coming of age of representational intelligence) is subphase specifically vulnerable. [p. 197]

Following these remarks, we presented brief case studies of two children who had participated in the separation-individuation study and in the follow-up interviews and psychological testing conducted during their early adolescence. We traced how each subphase makes its particular contribution to subphase adequacy, focusing on the three aspects of narcissism described by Spruiell—omnipotence, self-love, and self-esteem regulation. From there we went on to propose how superego and ego-ideal development might have been affected by imbalances in these three strands of narcissism.

Dramatic features in the separation-individuation process of both children were subphase inadequacies having to do with the vicissitudes of omnipotence and aggression. In one child, Sy, omnipotence was exaggerated at the expense of the object relations that contribute to self-love and self-esteem. With the other child, Cathy, a sudden deflation of omnipotence during rapprochement generated intensely ambivalent object relations, which in turn had the eventual effect of depleting Cathy's reserves of self-love and self-esteem.

In the case of Sy (pp. 198–203), the luxuriation of symbiosis prevented later subphases from making their specific positive contributions to personality development. The age-appropriate separate self- and body awareness was inundated by castration anxiety and overstimulation of fantasy life, which led to a distorted oedipal constellation and a deformation of ego-ideal and superego structures. In Cathy's case (pp. 204–208), "the narcissistic reserve, which might have enabled Cathy to overcome later narcissistic hurts, was depleted on two fronts during her practicing phase. The imbalance between Cathy's excessively exalted ego ideal and the relative paucity of phase-specific libidinal refueling during practicing proper" "laid the groundwork for inflexible ego-ideal and superego structures which would not allow for an adaptive tolerance for ambiguity and ambivalence" (p. 84).

In light of Mahler's commentary on the relations between subphase inadequacies and narcissistic imbalances, we might on some other occasion speculate about the fate of Erikson's virtues of will, purpose, and competence—all of which seem linked to individuation strivings and effective deployments of aggression.

ADOLESCENT OMNIPOTENCE AND THE CAPACITY FOR FIDELITY

Adolescence entails a deployment of personal narcissism into the impersonalized ideals that bind individuals to new family units, to the human community, and to the species. Fidelity, the vital virtue that emerges in the context of the larger psychosocial environment, transposes the issues of narcissism to another register of human experience. In exploring the meaning of fidelity, the distinctions between infantile narcissism and adolescent narcissism become evident.

It is not surprising that it has been more palatable for analysts, parents, and philosophers to focus on the early parent–child relationship. Infants and children are dependent and malleable. Much as they are crude and unformed in their sexual and moral nature, they hunger for regularity, boundaries, and stability. Parents are eager to encourage and abet the child's conformities. The love and devotion of the parents are a child's gentle seduction into civilization. However, at puberty, when the child's psychological separation from her parents entails the attainment of her own ego identity, and she must actually go her own way into her own life, the friendly relations between family life and civilization become highly equivocal.

To comprehend the meaning of fidelity we must engage the realm of social ideals and social values. The psychological issues that in childhood entailed primarily family dilemmas and parent–child attachments now at puberty begin to bring in a whole gamut of cultural dilemmas, particularly the quality and nature of an individual's attachment to society and civilization. Erikson (1959) warned against burdening the mother–child relationship with the entire responsibility for the child's moral life; and when he spoke of the connections between ego identity and omnipotence, he made a special point of distinguishing the familial and cultural levels of human existence:

> If [later] experience is to corroborate part of the infantile sense of omnipotence, then child training must know not only how to teach sensual health and progressive mastery, but also how to offer tangible social recognition as the fruits of health and

mastery. For unlike the infantile sense of omnipotence which is fed by make-believe and adult deception, the self-esteem attached to ego identity is based on the rudiments of skills and social techniques which assure a gradual coincidence of functional pleasure and actual performance, of ego ideal and social role. The self-esteem attached to the ego identity contains the recognition of a tangible future. [pp. 39–40]

And he warned that ego strength gains real strength in achievements that attain real meaning within culture. If the cultural environment deprives the adolescent of "the forms of expression which permit him to develop and to integrate the next step in his ego identity, he will resist with the astonishing strength encountered in animals who are suddenly forced to defend their lives" (pp. 89–90).

As I stated at the outset, rather than focus on the transformations of self-love and self-esteem, which, of course, also play a significant role in the capacity for fidelity, I will highlight adolescent omnipotence, the narcissistic transformation most closely related to regulations of aggression. As Mahler's work strongly suggests, transformations of narcissism and transformations of aggression are inextricably intertwined psychological issues. Henri Parens, whose theory of aggression evolved directly out of Mahler's separation-individuation studies, does not stress, as I do, the relationship between narcissism and aggression. And though we would both highlight the intimate relationship between affects and drive development, there are subtle differences between Parens's theory of drive development and mine. For example, by highlighting the reciprocity between the development of drives and object relations, I am also stressing that the libidinal object does not exist at birth and must be constructed. Furthermore, human drives (in contrast to animal instincts) are not innate—to develop they must be nurtured by the libidinal object. "In the absence of a reciprocal human dialogue, libido withers and never develops. In the absence of a reciprocating partner, an infant's aggressive strivings are simply chaotic and therefore urgently destructive" (Kaplan 1995, p. 23).

Nevertheless, I am comfortable with Parens's (1979, 1984) distinctions between the two trends of the aggressive drive, and would agree that both are discernible, at least in their incipient forms, within hours of birth—"non-destructive aggression," the product of an inborn system that serves adaptation, and "hostile destructiveness," which is activated by experiences of excessive unpleasure (1979, p. 270). Parens points out that hostile aggression can be a response to internal threats such as physical pain and distress, and in that connection asserts that the excessively felt unpleasure in a libidinally frustrating object relationship transforms aggression into a force with a "qualitative aim of inflicting pain and harm upon and of destroying the object" (1979, p. 111).

Summarizing the differences between Dollard's frustration-aggression hypothesis and his own theory of aggression, Parens (1991) reiterates:

> Excessive unpleasure of any source, not only frustration, generates hostile destructiveness even in earliest childhood. . . . This is so whether the unpleasure results from painful somatic stimuli (e.g., illness or injury), the frustration of libidinal needs, or of autonomy strivings. We shall elaborate . . . that several variables codetermine whether the unpleasure becomes experienced as excessive. The *meaning* to the self is a crucial variable. [p. 83]

Parens's writings focus on the unpleasures that are intrinsic to the separation-individuation process. I am making explicit those features of Parens's general formula that implicitly acknowledge the more complex psychological unpleasures that arise in later stages of human development, such as the oedipal and adolescent phases. During adolescence, the narcissistic humiliation that accompanies a libidinally frustrating object relationship is a major motive for transforming aggression into a destructive force. Furthermore, one outcome of the narcissistic humiliations that attend cultural deprivations is a hostile response to social reality. For example, in "On Narcissism," Freud (1914) stated that what the individual "projects before him as his ideal is [only] the substitute for the lost narcissism of childhood where he was once his own ideal" (p. 94)—and in the last paragraph suggested that paranoia may be an outcome of "a frustration of satisfaction within the sphere of the ego ideal" (p. 102).

During adolescence, cultural life can tame, hold, and contain what might otherwise be ruthless aggression, and thus facilitate those maturational processes whereby omnipotence and nondestructive aggression are enlisted in the service of culture and civilization. However, when the process of adolescence is accompanied by narcissistic mortification, then omnipotence and aggression can acquire the aims of inflicting pain and harm upon the object—the libidinal object, which in this instance is civilization itself. What we see is unbridled vandalism, attacks on public monuments, and outright homicide. And as we have learned all too well during this century, the "highest" of ideals can serve as an inspiration for exquisite sadism, holocaust, and genocide. As Freud (1914) cautioned, a person who has "exchanged his narcissism for homage to a high ideal has not necessarily on that account succeeded in subliminating his libidinal instincts" (p. 94).

The qualities—ego strengths or virtues—of intimacy and fidelity do not necessarily coexist. The personal life and the life of ideals are not necessarily commensurate. Indeed, in order to emphasize this point, I would even insist that fidelity concerns the capacity to impersonalize one's personal passions.

In one way or another, even though the precise words may elude them, adolescents ask themselves, "Is there something outside or beyond my personal everyday life that I might believe in?" What we hear, if we listen, are young people in search of something larger than ordinary, everyday existence—some ideals or values to which they might be true. The emergence of the vital virtue fidelity depends on youth being able to locate in the larger social order values or ideals that can accommodate their moral aspirations.

Erikson (1964) put the issues this way:

> Identity and fidelity are necessary for ethical strength, but they do not provide it in themselves. [Adults must] provide content for the ready loyalty of youth, and worthy objects for its need to repudiate. As cultures . . . enter into the fiber of young individuals, they also absorb into their life-blood the rejuvenative power of youth. Adolescence is thus a vital regenerator in the process of social evolution; for youth selectively offers its loyalties and energies to the conservation of that which feels true to them and the correction or destruction of that which has lost its regenerative significance. [p. 126]

Adolescence begins with crudities, simplifications, primitivizations of aggression, and narcissism—a breakdown of controls, an eruption of unruly passions and desires, a dissolution of the civilizing trends of childhood. Adolescents threaten adults with their sexual and moral intensities. In contrast to the innocent charm of infantile narcissism, the adolescent brand of narcissism is alarming and difficult for adults to appreciate, much less tolerate, because it is a direct challenge to an adult's self-esteem and power. It is hard to see any virtue in it at all.

I am reminded here of Pumpian-Mindlin's (1969) definition of adolescent "omnipotentiality."

> It [omnipotentiality] consists primarily of the feeling and conviction on the part of the youth that he can do anything in the

world, solve any problem in the world. . . . There is no occu-
pation which is inaccessible, no task which is too much for
him. As his perspective of the world broadens, as his horizon
widens, he begins to question everything his elders have come
to accept. . . . He knows no limits in fantasy, and accepts
grudgingly any limits in reality. [p. 222]

On the surface this description of adolescent omnipotentiality sounds very much like the omnipotence of the toddler
during the practicing proper subphase. Here and there
Pumpian-Mindlin seems to be subscribing to a recapitula-
tionist version of development, however essentially he
stresses the differences between infantile omnipotence and
adolescent omnipotentiality. In contrast to the adolescent
whose physical power and sexual potency pose real threats to
the adult generation, the toddler has no real power. The
toddler's sense of omnipotence is based on an unrealizable
fantasy, and as Mahler noted, infantile omnipotence is inevitably "shaken by the coming of age of representational intel-
ligence" (1977, p. 197). There is no similar natural outcome
for the taming of adolescent omnipotentiality. Adolescent
fantasies of power are potentially realizable, but actually possible only if they can be brought into harmony with the
demands of civilization. And for this transformation from
adolescent omnipotentiality to adult power and authority, the
young must begin by actively challenging the social and
cultural actualities that surround them. As Pumpian-Mindlin
(1969) asserts:

The free exercise of this omnipotentiality is a necessary and
salutary occurrence in youth. The wider the range of exploration, the more adequately prepared is the youth to relinquish
his omnipotential strivings and channelize them into specific
priorities, to choose the necessary, appropriate, inevitable
commitment. Unfortunately, adults, out of their own anxiety,
often make this essential exploration and experimentation as

difficult as possible for youth. The youth resent this and they
rebel against it . . . which leads to further repressive measures,
both social and individual. [p. 225]

Adolescence is an unsettling of the established order in
favor of an impassioned determination of new and as yet
untested ideals. Adolescents challenge our conservative ten-
dencies with their sexual and moral intensities, their aggressive explorations into new territories of experience, their
passionate pursuit of change and innovation. For all their
self-absorption and personalized aspirations, the young are in
pursuit of something larger than personal passions. Their
physical power, their procreative and creative abilities, their
visionary minds are ready to be directed toward the future of
civilization. Yet our modern world is haunted by the tremen-
dous waste of their moral potential. The guardians of youth—
parents and teachers, political and religious leaders—might do
well to ponder whether what they represent and convey as
social values and ideals will inspire fidelity in their charges or
encourage the perversities of narcissism that seem to be flourishing in our modern societies.

REFERENCES

Akhtar, S., Kramer, S., and Parens, H. (1995). *The Birth of Hatred.* Northvale, NJ: Jason
    Aronson.
Aries, P. (1960). *Centuries of Childhood: A Social History of Family Life,* trans. R. Baldick.
    London: Jonathan Cape, 1963.
_____ (1977). The family and the city. *Daedalus* Spring: 227–237.
Erikson, E. (1959). Ego development and historical change. In *Identity and the Life Cycle.* New
    York: International Universities Press.
_____ (1964). Human strength and the cycle of generations. In *Insight and Responsibility.* New
    York: W. W. Norton.
Flugel, J. C. (1921). *The Psycho-Analytic Study of the Family.* London: Hogarth Press.
Freud, S. (1905). Three essays on the theory of sexuality. *Standard Edition* 7:123–243.
_____ (1914). On narcissism. *Standard Edition* 14:67–102.

_____ (1920). Beyond the pleasure principle. *Standard Edition* 18:1–64.

_____ (1927). The ego and the id. *Standard Edition* 19:1–66.

_____ (1930). Civilization and its discontents. *Standard Edition* 21:59–145.

Kaplan, L. J. (1984). *Adolescence: The Farewell to Childhood.* New York: Simon and Schuster.

_____ (1995). *No Voice Is Ever Wholly Lost.* New York: Simon and Schuster.

Lasch, C. (1977). *Haven in a Heartless World.* New York: Basic Books.

Mahler, M. S. (1959). In collaboration with Paula Elkisch. On infantile precursors of the "Influencing Machine" (Tausk). In *The Selected Papers of Margaret S. Mahler,* vol. 1. New York: Jason Aronson, 1979.

_____ (1961). On sadness and grief in infancy and childhood: loss and restoration of the symbiotic love object. In *The Selected Papers of Margaret S. Mahler,* vol. 1. New York: Jason Aronson, 1979.

_____ (1966). Notes on the development of basic moods: the depressive affect. In *The Selected Papers of Margaret S. Mahler,* vol. 2. New York: Jason Aronson, 1979.

_____ (1967). On human symbiosis and the vicissitudes of individuation. In *The Selected Papers of Margaret S. Mahler,* vol. 2. New York: Jason Aronson, 1979.

_____ (1971). A study of the separation-individuation process and its possible applications to borderline phenomena in the clinical situation. In *The Selected Papers of Margaret S. Mahler,* vol. 2. New York: Jason Aronson, 1979.

Mahler, M. S., and Kaplan, L. J. (1977). Developmental aspects in the assessment of narcissistic and so-called borderline personalities. In *The Selected Papers of Margaret S. Mahler,* vol. 2. New York: Jason Aronson, 1979.

Mahler, M. S., Pine, F., and Bergman, A. (1975a). *The Psychological Birth of the Human Infant.* New York: Basic Books.

_____ (1975b). On the current status of the infantile neurosis. In *The Selected Papers of Margaret S. Mahler,* vol. 2. New York: Jason Aronson, 1979.

Parens, H. (1979). *The Development of Aggression in Early Childhood.* New York: Jason Aronson.

_____ (1984). Toward a reformulation of the theory of aggression and its implications for primary prevention. In *Psychoanalysis: The Vital Issues,* vol. 1, ed. J. Gedo and G. Pollock. New York: International Universities Press.

_____ (1991). A view of the development of hostility in early life. *Journal of the American Psychoanalytic Association* 39:75–108.

Pumpian-Mindlin, E. (1969). Vicissitudes of infantile omnipotence. *Psychoanalytic Study of the Child* 24:213–226. New York: International Universities Press.

Rousseau, J. J. (1755). Discourse on the origin and foundations of inequality. In *The First and Second Discourses,* ed. R. D. Masters, trans. R. D. and J. R. Masters. New York: St. Martin's Press, 1964.

Spruiell, V. (1975). Three strands of narcissism. *Psychoanalytic Quarterly* 44:577–595.

3

FIDELITY: FROM CANNIBALISM TO IMPERIALISM AND BEYOND

Discussion of Kaplan's Chapter "Transformations of Narcissism: From 'Omnipotentiality' to Fidelity"

Eric Lager, M.D.

In cultural terms, Louise Kaplan's response to the charge of discussing fidelity—to look at the fate of adolescent narcissism as it affects fidelity—is correct. Viewing this comparatively, adolescence is a problematic period in technologically advanced countries. In traditional cultures, where children contribute to the survival of groups, this critical period does not manifest itself with as much turmoil as in such contemporary groups. This period is analogous to the long dependency of human infants in comparison with other mammal newborns. In a sense, we humans are all born prematurely because of our large craniums, but we can go further in our development than other animals.

Similarly, adolescents in Western cultures are more exposed to narcissistic vulnerability because of our emphasis on individualism and preparation for future careers, but this allows them to go further in individual achievement. Robert and Ruth Monroe, in their book *Cross-Cultural Human Development* (1977), investigated the Trobrianders of Melanesia, the

49

Ainu of Japan, and the Gusii of East Africa. The Monroes suggest that the Western, more egalitarian structure fosters this kind of egoism, or narcissism. Male dominated, authoritarian, traditional societies quell a self-orientation in favor of the group. This may even manifest itself to the point where language does not provide the means for expressing self-awareness. We can look at this as a conflict of fidelity to self and the group with advantages and disadvantages in each.

Kaplan makes the point that safety in the environment is required for a trusting relationship to evolve between mother and child. Two prominent dangers are threats to the food supply and war, and these dangers shape cultures and their institutions. Kaplan states that the institutions of society make competing demands on a couple's fidelity. I am assuming that she is referring to military and religious institutions. I will discuss these further with regard to the past and the future.

The possibility for development of fidelity can be measured in a culture by the equality of men and women and the level of interest in the emotional development of children. A survey of our cultural history reveals that these have evolved mostly in this century. We are continuing to make progress toward equality as women enter the work force in increasing numbers. Engels (1891) predicted correctly over 100 years ago that women's economic independence would lead not to polyandry but to true monogamy.

Urbanization, however, takes working mothers out of the home and away from their children. With the pressures of time and money, it seems as if the golden age of interest in children has already peaked. Mahler's work (Mahler and Furer 1968, Mahler et al. 1975), rich and subtle in the study of interactions between mother and infant that promote object constancy and lead to the eventual possibility of fidelity, was a product of economic growth and prosperity in the industrial world. In a time of growing equality it will require the willing participation of fathers in their children's emotional development to support their growth toward freely given fidelity. It is possible that mastery over famine and war, at least on a large scale, will bring about the cultural change necessary to make this feasible.

FOOD, CHILDREARING, AND INSTITUTIONS

The demand for women's submission in certain patriarchal cultures must represent more than concern about spousal infidelity. A few weeks before this writing, Algerian women gathered in New York City and tried to understand why Islamic fundamentalists had dismembered and slit the throats of women in Algeria who chose not to wear veils in public. A less violent but also oppressive attitude was reported by an American correspondent in Somalia earlier this year. The correspondent quoted the country's most liberal newspaper publisher as stating categorically, "If a man kills a man, he owes the victim's family 100 camels; if he kills a woman, 50 camels." How did such cultural attitudes evolve?

Cultures are markedly influenced by food supply, which affects child rearing, which in turn perpetuates the cultures. The explanations for the dismemberment of women must also reflect these realities. Fundamentalist rhetoric of dismemberment by sword, the causing of blood to flow in holy wars, and the actuality of severed limbs from terrorist bombings is well known to us. The aggressive impulses are obvious.

What I am about to suggest is not the validity of a particular explanation but the relationship of child-rearing practices resulting from the exigencies of the particular surround as it reflects itself in the institutions and attitudes of a group. These relationships throw light on what would otherwise be unexplainable. Is it not possible that the continual slaughtering of animals in these highly meat-dependent

herding cultures in arid lands in front of little children develops in them a high level of anxiety that they will suffer the
same fate? For instance, the phrase "blood will flow" by the
sword of holy war is identical to the instruction for blood to
flow in ritual slaughter. A likely response for many is to turn
from passive observation to active participation and then to
displace the action to an outside group. This sharp distinction
between their group and others could represent a precocious
need for children to differentiate themselves from animals,
with which children usually identify well into the latency
period, and lead to a lack of empathy for other groups and for
those of the other sex. But these psychic determinants require
adaptive advantage for the community to support their expression in the culture, and this support is derived from
military and religious institutions. When these institutions
unite, we can expect a call for holy war. This kind of unity
derives from military success.

Cultures in which one sex or the other is dominant
produce a high rate of infidelity. Societies that have mother-
centered households tend to produce a great deal of male
infidelity and philandering. Most authoritarian cultures,
however, are patriarchies. They tend to produce female infidelity, even when to be unfaithful is to risk death. Certain
societies that are extremely male dominated, as in the Middle
East, tend to exaggerate differences between men and women
and devalue women and their role. Militarism, that is, the
need for men to risk their lives, supports patriarchy and the
valuing of men over women. Daughters are devalued.

Military adventurism supports extreme patriarchy and
becomes self-perpetuating if it is successful; if not, such societies can live for a time on memories of past glories. If,
however, adventurism continues to fail, other voices will be
heard, and not only moderating but reactive ones. They might
call for nonviolence or the prohibition of eating meat, for
example. To the degree that they succeed in being heard, they
will succeed in making institutions of their reforms.

FIDELITY IN HUNTING
AND GATHERING SOCIETIES

In attempting to understand culturally determined differences in spousal relationships, including fidelity, it is helpful to look backwards in time. Early peoples were hunters and gatherers. They lived communally, sharing belongings, especially food. Such groups, which exist even today, tend to be egalitarian, because women contribute vitally, and an authoritarian leader serves no purpose. Eskimo society, which still subsists by hunting, is such an example (Foulks 1995). The long prehistoric period of hunting and gathering is called the paleolithic age.

Planting and the domestication of animals was introduced in various parts of the world about 10,000 years ago. This, the neolithic period, lasted until about 2000 B.C. Agriculture brought private property, which stratified societies, including the relationships between men and women. Particularly in herding societies, from which present day Middle Eastern cultures are derived, men controlled the food supply and women were devalued. Wives were treated as property. Private property also brought slavery and plunder.

Surplus of food, however, permitted the development of cities and trade in the Bronze Age, beginning about 2000 B.C. It brought with it warfare, which is plunder on a large scale. About one thousand years later, during the Iron Age, imperialism evolved and further broke down the isolation of groups that still resembled primal man in their ways of subsistence.

For hunters and gatherers, there was no advantage in individual ownership. Property was for the user. Sharing usually included the communal raising of children. Since paternity was unknown, relationships were matrilineal. The mother's brother was responsible for her protection and that of her children. The father lived separately and provided this function for his sisters. These mother-centered groups were called clans. The Greeks called them gens, which was derived from the word "gyn" or woman. However, by the time they entered history, their clans had become patrilineal.

Marriage within the clan was usually taboo. It is likely that exogamy protected not only against strife within the clan over possession of women, but even more, it protected against attack by outsiders. Alliances with neighboring clans were made through exchange of women, intermarriage, but the women stayed with their own clan. Thus the man entered an alien clan where he risked being killed and even cannibalized in times of hunger. Eventually, alliances formed tribes with rudimentary and, of course, unwritten laws, but as the anthropologist Lewis Henry Morgan (1877), who lived with the Iroquois, found, what was outside the tribe was outside the law.

Marriage and fidelity were probably impermanent because the function of the husband was limited. Husbands were devalued by the men of the wives' clan. The courted woman might only accept a man who had undergone pubertal initiation as evidenced by circumcision or other mutilation such as tattooing or the knocking out of a tooth. This represented readiness to fight for the tribe and earned the right of passage through the territory of the allied clan. The Gusii, for instance, still refer to pre-circumcised boys, and for that matter, to pre-clitorectomized girls, in devaluing terms, but refer to boys who have undergone initiation as "circumcised man" or "warrior." Still, until recently in some societies, the suitor had to undergo humiliation at the hands of the future bride's kinswomen who smeared him with excreta, sexually attacked him, or otherwise forced him to accept a devalued position.

Devaluation of husbands resulted not only from uncertainty of paternity, but because there was a time when the physiological role of the father was unknown. The Monroes accept Bronislaw Malinowski's finding (1922) that the Trobrianders "recognize no connection between intercourse and pregnancy: They believe that a child is inserted into the mother's womb by the spirit of one of her dead kinswomen, and the father has nothing to do physiologically with the child . . ." (Monroe and Monroe 1977, p. 15). Thus the husband's role is diminished and men are devalued.

It is likely that warfare was compensatory for men who could not be as productive as women. In New Guinea, Tchambuli men tend to be passive, dependent, and probably depressed, but before the colonial administration forced them to give up the practice, they were headhunters.

Polygyny, the marriage of one man to more than one woman, also gave men status but was only available to the few who could afford to sustain a number of women and their children in those cultures that sanctioned it. Its purpose seems more social and economic, as seen in current transitional societies moving toward private property. The chief, or headman, has gained special privileges but also special responsibilities, both toward the women and his patriliny. This seems to reflect a willingness on the part of the group to imbue the chief with wisdom and magical power.

The circularity of child rearing practices and local ecologies put an indelible stamp on spousal relationships in prehistory and is reflected in more isolated cultures today. Reviewing studies on the child-rearing practices of the contemporary Aloresi of Indonesia, the Monroes found that they received very low scores for infant satisfaction and infant acceptance. Not surprisingly, they found that marriages were brittle and that adults showed a general tendency to give up easily and to be suspicious of each other.

In emphasizing the importance of the nature and quantity of food supply to the customs of peoples, the anthropologist and psychoanalyst Edward F. Foulks (1955) related a study that sought to determine what cultures that practice pubertal initiation rites have in common. All available data were entered into the computer for analysis, which revealed only one common variable: a low-protein diet. The explanation was that in these cultures mothers nurse their children until age 5, sometimes even up to age 9.

Fearing feminization of the boys, the men, usually living separately (in longhouses, for instance) seized the boys at puberty and put them through harsh initiation rites that tested them as hunters and fighters and also mutilated them in some way. Pubertal circumcision meant that boys belonged to the men and were ready to make further sacrifice if needed for the clan.

Thus, exogamy and initiation along with segregation became institutions at a communal level to deal with aggressive practices that made life too difficult to bear. As society advanced, such institutions came under the power of specialists, both military and religious. Circumcision became the covenant with God.

As patriarchy and patriarchal religion evolved in the Middle East, circumcision represented submission to God. Its performance at birth probably had more to do with infanticide than with humanitarianism. It is not accidental that Exodus depicts Moses' wife Zipporah quickly circumcising their son Eleazer in order to prevent God or Moses from slaying him in a moment of wrath. When Paul introduced the loving God of Christianity, he abolished circumcision but in turn required the man's continence, which both raised and lowered the place of women in society. Bergmann (1992) explained circumcision in the Middle East as a religious substitute for human sacrifice.

MILITARISM AND THE SEGREGATION AND DEVALUATION OF WOMEN

The bonding together of men as fighters requires the exclusion of women. In the early stages, the bands were clansmen who lived physically segregated from women. In nomadic herding tribes segregation was less possible because of the advent of private property. In these societies men controlled the protein supply of meat and milk, and women were treated like property. When the food supply became low, since finding grazing land was only somewhat more reliable than finding game, female infanticide came into vogue. This resulted in a paucity of wives, but it was more advantageous to steal them than to raise them (Divale and Divale 1976).

As city-states appeared and family life was strengthened, segregation diminished even further, but devaluation of women took its place. Segregation and devaluation counter the claim of women on men and strengthen the claim of men on men to fight to the death. To do otherwise would be to be like a woman.

The daily prayer of Orthodox Jewish men, thanking God that they were not born women, must counter the continual fear of the wish that had they been born women, they would not be exposed to such danger. When improved methods of warfare and mobility ushered in imperialism, pressures to maintain the separation of couples came from a centralized authority. These pressures were often political.

In pastoral societies, where crops could be planted and stored, women were valued and goddesses of fertility were worshiped. In the fertile Nile Valley there were probably priestesses who required the ritual sacrifice of the burning of the firstborn son (Daniel Freeman, personal communication, 1995). Apparently, such sacrifices to female goddesses were common in the fertile Middle East and took place during spring along with the sacrifice of the firstborn lamb. The Passover celebration, it is believed, derives from this tradition, as does the Jewish custom of "pidyon haben" (Bergmann 1992), representing the buying back of the firstborn son from the priest or priestess.

Until Cleopatra, the pharaohs of Egypt were matrilineally descended. The woman rule with the help of her brother and also her consort, whom she could dismiss or replace at will. Cleopatra's serial liaisons with Caesar and Antony were not out of the ordinary except that they were outsiders. As it happened, they did challenge the existing order. It was not until Octavian crushed it and turned Egypt into a Roman province to be exploited for its ample food supply that this matriarchy of thousands of years ended with the suicide of Cleopatra.

I speculate that it may have been just this dangerous mixture of personal love and political power with which the male ultimately dominated the woman and her clan that made men abjure handing power over to women, since it was men who ultimately faced the enemy and death. The matriarchal system insures this vulnerability because it allows the stranger, the potential enemy, into the matrilineal clan or tribe. Egyptian queens were not allowed to marry outside their clans. As societies became more open through travel and trade, this restriction became untenable. In the story of Samson and Delilah, Samson was a danger to the Philistines, who were patriarchal. A man entering a relationship with a woman in a matriarchy would have presented an even greater danger, as he would have shared his wife's power. This was particularly so if she was the queen. Patriarchy protects against this danger by ensuring that the wife goes to the husband's family, because women do not represent such a danger. This changeover from matriarchy to patriarchy is symbolized in the Old Testament declaration of Ruth to her mother-in-law, Naomi, "Whither thou goest, I will go."

Reed (1975), who has written extensively on the historical changeover from matriarchy to patriarchy, correctly interprets the myth of Medea as the tragedy of this changeover. Medea allows the adventurer-thief Jason into her matriarchal clan and assists him in stealing the golden fleece by murdering and dismembering her own brother. Fratricide was considered a more heinous crime than the murder of a husband who was not blood kin. Her murder of their sons and of his pregnant new wife, the queen, represents the greatest revenge she could exact by frustrating his most cherished wish, the establishment of his patriliny.

Yet there must be more to why this old myth appeared as the subject of a tragedy by Euripides at the end of the fifth century B.C. in Athens. The same can be said about the Agamemnon myth in the *Oresteia* by Aeschylus. In the *Oresteia,* Clytemnestra must die for killing her husband, Agamemnon, but her son is spared for killing her. In matriarchy, the killing of a husband, an outsider, is not as great a crime as the killing of a mother by her son, a blood relative. Both Aeschylus and Euripides were supporting the idea that the murder of these two powerful women was more justifiable than the murder of males in Athens. Athens was moving toward imperialism, and the continuing internecine wars against Sparta and others were sapping its life. All art in classical Greece was communal and chosen for political purposes, and these plays served the propaganda for war.

Curiously, the first legendary enemies of the Athenians were not Spartans but women. If the myths about Amazons represent history as well as unconscious fantasy, then there were in fact battles between men and women in the changeover from matriarchy to patriarchy. Such women warriors were described by the early anthropologist Diodorus in Roman times in Libya (Stone 1976). The prominence in mythology of battles of Athenians against the Amazons may mean they have historical significance. Again, a myth is used politically. A depiction of such a battle decorates Athena's shield as she stands gigantically in the new Acropolis, whose construction Pericles ordered on a brazen impulse. Using the tribute money of contributing states of the Delian League, he demonstrated the power of Athens over them.

Amazon in Greek means "without breast." It was said that these women amputated their right breasts so that they could better shoot their arrows. Such amputation has an aggressive implication similar to circumcision, and no doubt in the unconscious also represents oral aggression of men. Similarly, Indian depictions of Buddha, a contemporary, with a single woman's breast must represent oral aggression against the mother as well as Buddha's nurturance, both sides representing a reaction to how little is freely given in life. If there were battles between men and women, the men won; but in most cultures, the changeover came gradually.

The change from the institution of segregation and relative egalitarianism to the devaluation of women can be followed by comparing Spartan and Athenian societies. Although contemporary, Sparta was a virtual fortress enclosed by a wall of mountains beyond which the sea served as a moat and remained more traditional than Athens, which was exposed to the world, especially Asia. Athens was indeed a cosmopolitan polis or city.

Spartan social organization had remained more clanlike. Clan organization produces fierce fighters, though not the strategists and schemers of empires, and Sparta was, in fact, a military machine. It separated its young from their parents, the boys from the girls, and trained the young men to become fierce fighters. This culture produced nothing else, not even its own food. Prisoners taken in battle were forced into slavery exclusively for food production. Slaves outnumbered citizens ten to one and were communally owned and segregated, living in the fields they tended. They were systematically, publicly humiliated or even killed to instill the value that it is better to die in battle than to be a slave. Indeed, Spartans fought to their deaths until 400 B.C., yet women had higher status than they did in Athens, and this must have been because of segregation.

As previously noted, in Athens women were systematically devalued. Slaves were devalued by definition, but took part in the cultural life to which they contributed. Courtesans, called "hetaerae," who were educated slaves, fared better than wives. Domestic women slaves might serve as concubines, and children were raised with the wives' children. Men usually married women half their age, teenagers, who were handed over with a dowry, since the husband was taking over their support. This was so because the women had no useful work, that being done by slaves. The Greeks knew the connection between sex and procreation, but their theory fitted with their devaluation of women. In that theory, women served only as the containers in which men's germ plasm generated children.

Athenian men did not come to take their sons from their mothers into forced initiation. They seduced them away at the symposia, exclusive to men (with the exception of female slaves), where ample wine was drunk and intellectual discussion took place. Older men took younger men in tow. This often included homosexual relations. Engels (1891) believed that it was the devaluation of women that led to homosexuality, but we know that the initiation rites of primitives also include homosexual acts. From a developmental point of view, when boys are segregated from their fathers with their mothers, they will develop homosexual longings. The Monroes find a correlation between absent fathers and the glorification of warfare. Male bonding for military purposes was a deliberate policy. As the city of Thebes ascended militarily, it developed an elite corps of 300 fighters. They comprised 150 couples of homosexuals, an older and a younger man, out of the correct belief that when men fight out of love, they fight better than out of hate.

How is it possible that the role of women had fallen even from the time of the *Odyssey,* in which Penelope is Odysseus's female counterpart? The *Iliad* and *Odyssey* were written down some 300 years before the period I am describing, and these myths refer to events some 700 years before. Perhaps women had not fallen at all. In the *Iliad* women are treated as nothing

but property to be fought over by men. In the *Odyssey,* which
may be the greatest ode to fidelity ever written, women are
portrayed so differently that the keenly psychological novelist
Samuel Butler suggested that it was not Homer who was its
author but his daughter.

There is a larger truth in Butler's idea despite the fact that
scholars do not take it seriously. In Greece a woman could
have written the *Odyssey.* Whatever the shortcomings of
Greek civilization, it produced a golden age in which women
were not crushed. The propaganda, the systematic and even
philosophical devaluation of women, represented a dynamic
imbalance. In other cultures, in contrast, the balance was
fixed, with little of cultural value produced. It has been said
that the Greeks attained their golden age because slaves did all
the necessary work, but creativity, we know, requires a dissolution of barriers, a blending of male and female functions,
as well as a blending of many cultures and their institutions.

In the meantime, Jews under and probably because of
successive subjugations including the Greeks under Alex-
ander the Great had, against persistent opposition even of
their own people, brought an end to human sacrifice, slavery,
and polygamy. No doubt their food rituals, as well as those of
other major religions, derive from overcoming human sacrifices, including earlier cannibalism. Their portable male god
served a nomadic people that originally had no tie to a specific
mother earth. This was a god easily adaptable to peoples of the
arid Arabian peninsula who spread swiftly over a considerable
part of the known world, beginning at about 700 A.D., having
been converted to Islam if not by belief, then by the sword.

The derision and dehumanization of those who sub-
mitted to Islam, while others died in defending the mother-
land, serves today, 500 years after the Turks converted
Christians in Bosnia, as a justification for greed and power-
seeking. The killing of men, and the raping and killing of
women and children, represents the return of early barbarism
only thinly veiled by moral religion that never significantly

altered old child-rearing practices, as a native psychologist of that region has pointed out.

FIDELITY AND ORIGINAL SIN

Religion that serves only magical needs without promulgating ethical principles, which are in essence maternal and life affirming, must eventually destroy its own culture. Examples are the religions of pre-Columbian South America, cultures that had otherwise reached high levels of barbarism. One can imagine that their priesthood called for increasingly greater human sacrifice, "blood must flow," to explain why their gods had not responded favorably to their pleas. In the fifteenth century, shortly before the European conquest, the Incas sacrificed as many as 80,000 lives each year. It has been proposed that other cultures of that region perished because of this priestly top-heaviness, despite the call for externalized aggression.

All ethical religions demand sacrifice, usually in the form of self-denial; and the more under pressure from external forces, the greater this self-denial must be if it is clear that aggression turned outward is hopeless. If the enemy is not relentless, this self-denial becomes a moral moderating force in opposition to the aggressor.

This must have been what happened in the Middle East as ascetic Jewish sects such as the Essenes developed under Roman domination. It is out of these sects that Christianity evolved. Paul persuaded his followers to imitate Christ, a loving and self-denying man. Christ, like Buddha 600 years before, probably had no mother but was himself maternal.*

---

*Early Christian writings, in stressing his divinity, followed Hebrew tradition that the Messiah would appear from nowhere. As late as 100 A.D., the Epistles to the Hebrews, a section of the New Testament, reiterates, "He has no father, no mother, no lineage" (Grant 1977).

The similarity between Christ and Buddha is so striking that many Hindus and Buddhists explain the blackout in the legend of Christ's life between his birth and his appearance as savior by the idea that during that time Christ was in India.

Self–denial included sexual abstinence. This requires segregation. Paul interpreted the sin of Adam and Eve as sexual and connected Christ's self-sacrifice with expiations for sex or original sin, a doctrine that was to have a profound impact on men's view of women, in order to at least attempt segregation. Eve then becomes the temptress in subsequent Western history. The Old Testament story is more ambiguous, and Eve probably was derived from an earlier goddess, a forerunner of Isis, who was also depicted as a serpent. The pacifism of Christianity eliminated the military motive for the devaluation of women and indeed, in the early Church, women participated actively. Christianity continued to exert a moral force for spousal fidelity from then on.

The Old Testament story of the loss of Paradise begs to be interpreted along evolutionist lines rather than as sexual sin. The Garden of Eden can be none other than the preserve of an earlier regional hunter-gatherer society, where food was mainly gathered or picked off trees. Although early hunters and gatherers did not have the knowledge that copulation results in pregnancy, this knowledge was essential for the domestication of animals. It also brought about restriction of sexual freedom.

The discovery of the intercourse-procreation connection was almost as empowering as the earlier discovery of the making of fire (Reed 1975). Primitives often do not understand natural causes, including those of life and death, and may ascribe them to magic or the gods. The fear of retaliation by the gods once humans become empowered is inevitable, as seen in the punishment of Prometheus in the Greek myth.

That Adam and Eve were punished by expulsion implies the evolutionary explanation that hunter-gatherers were displaced by herders and planters. The story tells us that Cain and Abel, the sons of Adam and Eve, were respectively the first tiller of the soil and the first herder. But herding and tilling are hard work, especially in contrast to living off a fertile oasis, idealized retrospectively. The biblical writer was saying, in essence, "Do not blame God for the sweat of your brow, blame man, or better yet, blame woman, blame Eve." Again, herein is a truth: women, not men, would have had to be the first to make the connection between intercourse and pregnancy. The serpent is the symbol for the messenger and for knowledge, as it is in Greek mythology. Ironically, women's great discovery brought about barbarism with its patriarchal domination of them and the elimination of female gods.

We are familiar with the idea that religions oppose the promulgation of the knowledge of natural causes because the power of religions derives from their priests' exclusive access to purported wisdom. The combination of an antiinformation and antisexual attitude, along with the demand for complete faith in authority to which the ordinary person's acknowledged sinfulness is the necessary counterpart, itself derives from the peculiar origins of Christianity. This association permitted the central authority to continue even after the fall of Rome. Authority was inherent in the Roman family. The Roman paterfamilias had the right to kill his wife for infidelity. He also had the right to kill or sell into slavery not only his children but his grandchildren. Christ on the cross, abandoned by his father, was not merely a poignant symbol for humankind.

The romanization of Christianity can be seen as representing opposing attitudes toward women. The appearance of the Virgin must have been the reincarnation of a pagan goddess. Athena was a virgin, as was Artemis. This female permeation of patriarchy had to be virginal according to the doctrine of original sin. Yet the centralized patriarchal control of the church was a continuation of Roman imperialism. If militarism required patriarchy in Rome, what could justify it for the mother church? The doctrine of original sin in which the woman is the seducer sets the stage for a centralized authority. If man is inherently sinful, then patriarchal control is required (David Laney, personal communication, 1995).

In comparison with the powerful Roman patriarchy, the barbarian Germanic tribes still under clan organization were egalitarian in their attitude toward women, and the intermingling that followed the fall of Rome improved the stature of women. The higher status of women among the Germans must have derived in part from the custom of women coming on the battlefields to cheer their men on. We are familiar with the helmeted Valkyries in Richard Wagner's opera *Die Walküre* who rode onto the fields to gather the fallen heroes. In Germany in the eleventh century a woman could dissolve a marriage for as little reason as the foulness of her husband's breath. On the other hand, boys suffered great cruelty. At the time of the codifying of these marriage laws, the main exports of one German town were eunuchs for the harems of Spain. The persistence of clan structure in northern Europe must also explain some differences between Protestantism and Catholicism. In the first, despite the absence of the Virgin cult, women are more prominent in the church, and priests can marry. Also, the Protestant Church has seen many schisms, whereas the Roman Catholic Church maintains its imperial character.

If harsh patriarchy produces infidelity, or at least the desire for it in women, then harsh mothers and wives do so in men as well. At about 400 A.D. St. Augustine founded the first Christian monastic order and instituted celibacy for his followers. He had been converted to Christianity under the influence of his strong-willed mother after being a compulsive philanderer, as he recounts in his *Confessions*. Celibacy has been called the "A.A. cure" of total abstinence; the readiness to abstain from gratification of strong instinctual urges under the guidance of a leader whose love is sought conveys power to the leader.

This relationship no doubt did not escape the attention of the popes, or "papas," who instituted celibacy for the priesthood about 600 years later, at a time when Europe was emerging from the dark ages. As both food and safety increased, Virgin cults began to appear, and these eventually led to the urge to build huge cathedrals to Our Lady ("Notre Dame"). But celibacy ensured the exclusion of women, an extreme segregation, from influence in the church and increased its power over its ministers. How else could an empire be administered without engendering countless infidelities? Another motive for prohibiting priests to marry was economic. It was cheaper to support a single man. Probably the church needed money at that time because of increasing involvement in warfare against Moslems, such as in the Crusades.

In Ireland however, Celtic clan culture persisted into the seventeenth century, until that nation's domination by the English under Cromwell (Engels 1891). Matriarchy had taken its firmest stand in Europe there for this and for economic and political reasons. The land yields its fruit grudgingly, and considerable herding is required. Because of this, and also because the English landowners made little capital investment, farmhands were drawn from among the children of the working families. Procreation, and therefore motherhood, was valued. Large families required the mother to administer rather than to minister, appointing an older daughter as caretaker of siblings and of caretaker of herself in her old age. One son might be designated for the priesthood as the rigid adherence to Catholicism was a powerful political statement against the patriarchal Protestant English oppressors. It found confluence in the antisexuality of the doctrine of original sin, which permits sex only for procreation.

Nevertheless, one of the sons might fall between the cracks, be designated as the black sheep, or become a philanderer. The word *philanderer* comes from the Greek for "lover of men" and means to wander, and there is much truth in this. The wandering medieval minstrels are credited with the invention of romantic love, which was temporary if not tragic and usually adulterous. What *was* shameful was breach of loyalty to men, to bands of "brothers."

The configuration of Irish matriarchy was illustrated in Friel's (1991) wistful play about his childhood, *Dancing at Lughnasa*. A young boy lives with his mother and spinster aunts who want to go to the annual dance but dare not because their deceased mother forbade it. The boy's father is a philanderer and appears for a brief visit. The boy and his mother are happy to see him. He dances with the mother and leaves. The women then break into a wild tribal war dance, while the old uncle recently returned from long service in Africa intones an African tribal ceremonial which resonates with his own Irish clan roots.

Powerful European states, however, were more susceptible to the desire for empire. Napoleon, who was Italian but dropped the Italian-sounding "u" from Buonaparte, clearly identified himself with Roman emperors. His legal code explicitly permits a husband to have affairs as long as he does not bring his mistress into the home. The wife is not given the same privilege, but the inevitability of her doing so is provided for in that offspring from such a union belong to the husband. This is a return to bride price, in which a man purchased a wife not the least for her progeny, which belonged to him no matter what happened to the marriage. This practice is still enforced in the Middle East and permits taking another wife, either through addition or exchange, if the first produces no son. An Islamic divorce requires only the husband's pronouncement "I divorce you." The Napoleonic Code was consistent with the way of life of an imperialist militarism in which fidelity was impossible. The Nazis tried to inculcate similar values with regard to women when the Germans made their reach for empire.

The accepted practice in France of the husband having both a wife and mistress allows for a psychic split, which reduces the demand on the husband to achieve psychological object constancy. Otto Rank, in our century, said he had to leave France because he was unable to develop a psychoanalytic practice there—the custom of having mistresses allowed men to have relationships that could bypass neurosis and psychic pain. Why did this custom not fill his waiting room with women? Probably because under these circumstances women lived more or less in extended matriarchal families, in this way not having to effect separation-individuation, like the girls in matrilocal clans, and, like them, taking serial lovers, often initiating young men into sexuality.

The matriarchy of poor African Americans is another example of one sex, in this case men, denied economic equality and fallen in status in the family and society. Segregation means devaluation. The absence of fathers that is a hazard of the resultant serial monogamy, and the often harsh treatment of children of the poor in general, contributes further to the perpetuation of a cycle in which children are not prepared for their future in a technological world either educationally or emotionally through an adequate separation-individuation phase.

CONCLUDING REMARKS

Kaplan's seemingly paradoxical observation that utopianists have been opposed to the family must relate to their search for sexual freedom. Wilhelm Reich, for instance, looked to Malinowski's work on the Trobrianders (Malinowski 1922) to support the possibility of sexual freedom, even though he knew they were a society that had not yet discovered sexual paternity. The knowledge of the causation of pregnancy restricts sexual freedom, which in a society that values equality and intimacy in the couple can only eventuate in fidelity, contraception, and protected sex notwithstanding.

Clearly the work of Mahler (Mahler and Furer 1968, Mahler et al. 1975) as it relates to fidelity in the nuclear family cannot be overestimated. Its extension into the present and future will require studies of children with caretakers in addition to the mother, especially the father, in our culture. The exposure of cultures to each other will have moderating effects on extremes of variation in child rearing. Greater economic equality between fathers and mothers, as well as greater economic equality among classes and nations, will reduce the likelihood of wars, which in turn will enhance the possibility for greater fidelity between man and wife. The forces against these are, however, formidable. The dangers are greed and hunger for power, which result not from material need, but from poorly negotiated childhood development.

REFERENCES

Bergmann, M. S. (1992). *In the Shadow of Moloch: The Sacrifice of Children and Its Impact on Western Religions.* New York: Columbia University Press.

Divale, W., and Divale, H. (1976). Population, warfare, and the male supremacist. *American Anthropologist* 78:521–538.

Engels, F. (1891). *The Origin of the Family, Private Property and the State.* New York: Pathfinder, 1975.

Foulks, E. F. (1995). Personal communication.

Friel, B. (1991). *Dancing at Lughnasa.* London: Faber and Faber.

Grant, M. (1977). *Jesus: An Historian's Review of the Gospels.* New York: Charles Scribner's Sons.

Mahler, M., and Furer, M. (1968). *On Human Symbiosis and the Vicissitudes of Individuation. Volume I. Infantile Psychosis.* New York: International Universities Press.

Mahler, M., Pine, F., and Bergman, A. (1975). *The Psychological Birth of the Human Infant.* New York: Basic Books.

Malinowski, B. (1922). *Argonauts of the Western Pacific.* New York: Dutton.

Monroe, R., and Monroe, R. (1977). *Cross-Cultural Human Development.* New York: Jason Aronson.

Morgan, L. H. (1877). *Ancient Society, or Researches in the Lines of Human Progress from Savagery through Barbarism to Civilization.* London: Macmillan.

Reed, E. (1975). *Woman's Evolution: From Matriarchal Clan to Patriarchal Family.* New York: Pathfinder.

Stone, M. (1976). *When God Was a Woman.* New York: Dorset.

4

INTIMACY AND INDIVIDUATION

Alvin Frank, M.D

Intimacy, "the quality or condition of being intimate" (*Compact Oxford English Dictionary* 1991, p. 869) is one of those special words that attracts a host of meanings. The *Oxford English Dictionary* lists an even dozen. Through its common elements, closeness and familiarity, intimacy conveys the sense of a gamut of identifiable phenomena involving two or more persons. Here lie the roots of its positive connotations for us as mental health professionals. We believe, with reason, that a life without intimacy is a life robbed of the sublime. Similarly, without the building blocks of intimate gratification in development, we cannot conceive of a healthy and fulfilling adult life. When Bruno Bettelheim (1969) published his study of Israeli kibbutzniks raised impersonally, sans intimacy, it mattered little to most of us that they grew up to be splendid team players, cooperative workers, or fighter pilots. It was their reported lack of the capacity or need for fulfilling closeness that got our attention.

When limited to the psychological realm, as here, intimacy applies to a succession of interrelated yet distinct experiences. Observation confirms that the intimacy of the nursing dyad (breast and mouth) is distinct from that of the potty pair, that sought by the oedipal suitor, or that of a school friendship; it is distinct from the intimacy of the Romeos and Juliets of adolescence, of young adult commitment and passion, of the closeness within a family (in addition to between its individual members), or that of growing old together. And yet each has a definable common essence. Intimacy at any given time is not as elemental an emotional state as we sometimes treat it. It is more complex, a combination and product at different times of different ingredients. Its flowerings follow a step-by-step progression, as implied above, each phase specific. It has a developmental line. And each way stop has, as well as its hallmarks, its own anxieties and pathology.

The psychoanalytic literature does not treat the experiences of intimacy per se extensively.[1] Its psychoanalytic characterization and definition are not included in either edition of Moore and Fine's *Psychoanalytic Terms and Concepts* (1968, 1990), or Laplanche and Pontalis (1973). Anna Freud and her group did not assign it a developmental line. Earlier analytic authorities usually treated it as a one-stop experience, that of young adult to early-middle-age heterosexual consummation in the context of genital primacy (Rycroft 1968). Erikson (1968) stated that it is "only when identity formation is well on its way that true intimacy—which is really a counterpointing as well as a fusing of identities—is possible" (p. 135). He (1950) limited it to one-half of the nuclear conflict of the sixth of his eight stages of man, intimacy versus isolation:

1. The *Computer Index Title Key Word and Author Index to Psychoanalytic Journals,* covering almost three quarters of a century (1920–1994), has only five explicit references to *intimate* and *intimacy*. By way of comparison, the broader-based PsycINFO includes 919 such title citations in the roughly eleven-year period from 1984 to April 1995.

It is only as young people emerge from their identity struggles that their egos can master the sixth stage, that of intimacy. What we have said about genitality now gradually comes into play. Body and ego must now be masters of the organ modes of the nuclear conflicts, in order to be able to face the fear of ego loss in situations which call for self-abandon: in orgasms and sexual unions, in close friendships and in physical combat, in experiences of inspiration by teachers and of intuition from the recesses of the self. The avoidance of such experiences because of a fear of ego loss may lead to a deep sense of isolation and consequent self-absorption. [p. 229]

His requirements and criteria for the attainment of intimacy are largely subsumed in his ideas of genitality, with the orgasm its essence and model. It is the fusion, that is, merger, that accompanies orgasm that constitutes the threat of ego loss:

Genitality, then, consists in the unobstructed capacity to develop an orgastic potency so free of pregenital interferences that genital libido is expressed in heterosexual mutuality, with full sensitivity of both penis and vagina, and with a convulsion-like discharge of tension from the whole body. To put it more situationally: the total fact of finding, via the climactic turmoil of the orgasm, a supreme experience of the mutual regulation of two beings in some way breaks the point off the hostilities and potential rages caused by the oppositeness of male and female, of fact and fancy, of love and hate. [p. 230]

In something of an expansion of this view Binstock (1973) recognized the intimacies of both the mother–child dyad and adult heterosexuality. In each "there is a yearning and striving toward a kind of fusion with each other, . . . an urge to merge" (pp. 93–94). In agreement with Erikson, both relationships are expressions of bodily need, and Binstock, too, considered genitality as the exemplar of adult intimacy. He posited an ongoing dialectic between the two intimacies, to the potential detriment or advantage of the subjects depending on whether the product was regressive or integrative.

But the developmental literature of roughly the last eleven years, as represented in the broader-based PsycINFO, cited earlier, differs sharply with these narrow characterizations. In particular, the findings of developmental psychology contribute to the view of intimacy as an evolving, stepwise process, as proposed earlier. Intimacy and its pathology are considered in young childhood, schoolchildren, adolescence, adult friendship, and middle age; between men, in narcissists, in the life cycle, in families (including those with chemically dependent, abusive, and incestuous features), and in adoptees. And the early emphasis on its somatopsychologic essence is diluted by consideration of a variety of generative, purely psychologic, experiential factors. There are also nine papers about intimacy in the psychoanalytic situation and process, a phenomenon long recognized by practitioners.

Because intimacy is an experience involving two or more people, a developmental and genetically determined phenomenon, the status of each party's psychic structures is an inescapable consideration. My focus in this chapter is on the vicissitudes, and a particular instance of the pathology, of individuation as shaping the experience of intimacy. I use individuation as defined by Mahler and colleagues (1975, p. 4): It "consists of those achievements marking the child's assumption of his own individual characteristics." In Mahler's separation-individuation reciprocity usually the first is the more visible; it is demonstrably easier to correlate behavior with observable comings and goings than with inferred structural evolution. So the material I will cite is an opportunity to see the other side of the coin more clearly than usual.

CASE PRESENTATION[2]

A young man, embarking on his career, began therapy and then analysis because he longed to have sexual or intimate relations with a person and had been unable to do so because he was so frightened. He had a history of other disruptive and disabling anxiety symptoms, including obsessional and phobic features, since the age of 7. An occasional thread was a terror that he would not be able to direct his physical actions. He feared that in a variety of situations he would lose control of himself, run amok, and might hurl himself into an obstacle.

He was incapable of any intimate relationship, let alone action, appropriate to his time and place. In contrast, he did seem to be reasonably well liked in superficial interaction with peers and co-workers. Although apparently considered attractive and occasionally approached invitingly by women, he was a virgin. When a woman made her availability clear, he would withdraw. As an adolescent he had gotten into bed with a young woman, a contemporary. He had expected playful rubbing and giggling, but to his surprise she began to respond more seriously, and he felt his own excitement mount. He bolted from the bed in panic. He worried about whether he was gay, and sometimes found himself stimulated by men. In fact, he could become very aroused with a man or a woman. He was concerned by his appearance, and regarded himself as seeming very young as well as effeminate, without reason. He said he wasn't sure whether he felt he was a boy (which to him has feminine connotations), a man, or a woman.

A feature of his treatment was that when he was emotionally in a homosexual posture, his dreams and productions showed heterosexual anxieties, and vice versa. In fact, his first homosexual fantasies occurred in an adolescent group situation where he was frightened by several girls turning on to him. But he had little elective contact with either men or

_____

2. The material presented is derived from reasonably recent memory, process notes, and summaries at the times of reporting. There is no falsification of data.

women. His weekends were spent mostly in his apartment, alone, masturbating. The flat was modeled after his parents', and he cared for it with the same goal of total cleanliness as his mother did hers. The prospect of someone visiting his home filled him with dread. In the course of the analysis it became clear that he viewed his quarters as an extension of himself so concretely that the impact of a guest would mean the loss of his self. Similarly, the prospect of his genitals entering another's body, a man's or a woman's, or of another's bodily part entering him, would mean that the others had lost their separateness and taken his. This included castration anxiety but was, still more, the fear of losing his identity.

This man's one friend as he began treatment was a highschool chum, in most ways a clone. His pal was also sexually inexperienced, socially immature, and isolated. On one hand he filled the patient with contempt, and the patient was embarrassed to be seen with him. But he was his one real friend, the only one he went out with. They constantly compared and contrasted themselves with each other. Any perceived difference was the source of immediate anxiety and envy. When this person did become seriously involved with a woman, the patient angrily ended the friendship, only eventually returning in a much more measured and distant, although gracious, manner. He described himself as shattered and destroyed. It was for him a clear infidelity, a betrayal of their intimacy. It never again could be, and wasn't, the same. But in a short while the patient found himself another near double, a man, just a bit more different from himself than his predecessor, and idealized rather than disparaged. Again, anxiety-laden comparison was conspicuous from the first moments of closeness. It was this infatuation that led to his first, on and off, adult sexual relationship with another, limited to necking and mutual masturbation. There were two anxieties associated with their encounters, one of which the patient mastered and the other of which inhibited his full sexual expression. The first was the problem of his lover entering his home for their trysts. With effort he could tolerate this. The second was his excited desire that his partner enter his body anally. This he could not permit himself, and he ruthlessly controlled this impulse. Yet their orgasms through manual stimulation did not seem to pose a problem. They both believed that through their shared sexuality each would gain the ability to have a relationship with a woman. Hence, the twinning included the fact of each regarding himself as unformed and in process. But even with this experience he had the same questions about his own identity: boy, man, or woman, and the desired gender of his lover. He still had no clear idea of what he wanted for himself or a sexual partner.

The patient did well symptomatically as analysis went on. He seemed to use the experience in such a way that he could function more effectively, particularly in his work life and casual relationships, and was less troubled by anxieties and the symptoms they occasioned. Yet the ameliorative factors were not clear. There was no convincing evidence of object transference or its resolution.

Similarly, although the patient continued to reveal more of himself and his life, there was not a significant deepening of his presentation as a psychological being. For example, he did not demonstrate that his wishes for men and women were inherently in conflict, and that their alternation was the result of the ascendant wish invoking its counterpart as an assertion of its own power. Rather, he continued to present himself as unformed and lacking enough of a sense of himself to really know or feel what he really was or wanted. Forward thrusts led to so much anxiety that he would counter and undo them by asserting the opposite.

The meaning and impact of the analyst were muted, except under one circumstance, his absences. During those times the patient constructed an agenda of defined personal tasks, including consummated heterosexual intercourse, to be completed immediately. In these impassioned surges to completeness he put himself in situations ordinarily regarded as unapproachable. There he hoped his successful performance would indicate his own selfness through obviation of his symptoms and the problems that underlay them. These efforts were rarely successful; he dared far less than his checklist included, and his triumphs were confined to relatively unimportant areas and counted for little in the long run.

DISCUSSION

Before going on to how he got this way, I'd like to share some surmises about this man's individuation status. He walked a tightrope. While terrified by the prospect of losing himself and his control over functions as fundamental as muscular control, he could not tolerate the anxiety of further differentiation. The corresponding anxiety about progressive individuation in children is a cornerstone of separation-individuation theory (Mahler et al. 1975, p. 103). His pathologic compromise was twinship, where he could simultaneously have the experience of intimacy as being involved with another as a clone, and the reassurance of separateness as one of a pair. In part this involved the symbolic status of his "twin" having the meaning of an alter ego. But its enactment involved more than not contradicting that idea. It was a functional necessity. He needed this believed identical other to participate with him in order to experience and perform in life. On the one hand, any difference between himself and his twin threatened their unity. On the other, any true intimacy, which for him included physical entrance from, or into, the other, meant he was no more. Here is a clear demonstration of his concretism. The idea of intimacy as a psychological happening was still married to that of bodily union, the undeveloped belief system of an infant or young child. It was not that sexual intercourse could exemplify and express psychological intimacy, it was that it *was* the latter. The relevant symbolic representations were simply lacking. This contributes to understanding his problem with guests. His home did not symbolize his body—he deeply felt it as equivalent. The interpretation "You fear visitors because it's as if they are entering your body as they cross the threshold" could not have a curative impact on the basis of the patient recognizing his anxiety as symbolically rather than realistically based. It would rather be experienced as a mere clarification of his reaction to something very real to him.

This man was unsure of his gender because his gender was unsure, undifferentiated. His individuation was so arrested that he was not psychically child or adult, he or she, let alone capable of deciding whether to want him or her. Sexual situations or stimulation with either a woman or a man were avoided, fled from, or undone through fantasizing sexual involvement with the other gender. Yet, contrary to Erikson and others, orgasm as part of bodily union was not one of the experiences that meant fusion and loss of self. It was letting someone else through the front door or into his body that frightened him. Perhaps this seeming discrepancy is partially due to the possibility that sexual climax had no or little symbolic meaning to him.

But the transference experience was not the identity through twinship that the patient sought in his everyday life. This was confirmed by the observed unimportance of differences from, or similarities to, the analyst. It provided a different dimension of psychic completeness. It was as if the analyst fulfilled an intrapsychic function, as if he were those ego capacities consistent with a more advanced degree of individuation and higher level of functioning. Originally defined by Kohut (1971) as pertaining to the regulation of self-esteem, the idea of the selfobject relationship and transference has been broadened (Goldberg 1989, Lichtenberg 1991, Stolorow 1986) to include "another person who is performing a necessary psychic function for the self" (Goldberg, p. 204), as here.

PAST HISTORY

Let me now return to the patient's history, which I hope will contribute to the understanding of both the origins and characteristics of his adult psychopathology. In the interest of space I will organize this presentation to demonstrate the circumstances that impeded normative individuation. They include the rejections and deprivations of him as he was and should have been expected to become; the pressures, seductions, and stimulations that led to arrests and pointed him in other directions; and the profound anxieties whose existence further discouraged his individuation.

He is the elder of two children. The younger, a sister, was born a few months after his first birthday. His birth was considered a tragedy; his parents wanted a girl. Family legend has it that his father apologized to his mother, taking the blame as if the parenting of a boy were his failure. His mother was the dominant parent, described as demanding, strict, cold, and unpredictably enraged. Even aside from this the patient felt that her treatment of him was in many ways identical with that of his sister, that she could not distinguish between him as a boy and his sister as a girl. At the same time there was a special relationship between the women in the family that could not be matched by that between the men or between women and men. Also, men were subordinated to women. In fact, the patient's career choice was made by his mother despite his lack of interest and his fervent attraction to an entirely different field.

The patient has a screen memory that he associates with his mother being away having his sister. His maternal grandmother and aunt were standing over him while he was very upset, looking at him. The message is unmistakable. He is alone, distraught and helpless. Those who he would expect to comfort and succor him stand apart, coldly observing. Behind the unavailable grandmother and aunt one must infer the absent mother, who has deserted him in favor of the sister she prefers.

The two children grew up in the closest affinity, and shared a room until he was 7. They played many excited games together, giggling, jumping into each other's beds, and talking with their stuffed animals. He reports that they felt very much like a couple and were inseparable. This was encouraged by an explicit ethic: closeness within the family, through one's entire lifetime, and over generations, was an ultimate good. The analytic record strongly suggests that they probably showed each other their genitals, perhaps around 3 or 4. They also played an exciting game of simulated intercourse using the stuffed animals. When the patient moved into his own room, he had the first intimations of his adult phobias; he feared there was something in the closet or something coming through the window. He himself attributed his symptoms to an auto accident later that same year. He was thrown forward out of control, and a young girl was left bleeding. His recollection of this experience is remarkably similar to that of the earlier screen memory. It is of faces, of adults, looking down at him from outside. But in this memory the individual faces are ambiguous, confusingly both male and female. Again there is the theme of injury, now physical. The force beyond his control is again external, leaving him a victim of others. The adults are still, repetitiously, distant and not engaged. There is a repeated reference to his sister, through the young girl. What does the mention of her injury signify? Certainly his underlying rage and wish to destroy, but it also condenses his fear of her loss. And her bodily injury condenses his own, amounting to castration. The theme of his own gender confusion is manifest, introduced through projection onto the onlookers.

From about this time the patient believes himself to have been plagued by a multitude of anxieties and obsessions. Yet, outwardly, he seemed to be doing more than reasonably well. He was apparently involved with schoolmates, accepted, excelled scholastically, and participated in the expected activities except when they were precluded by symptomatology, such as stage fright.

With puberty, and well into his adulthood, his father became increasingly demonstrative and affectionate toward him. He hugged him, kissed him on the lips, called him "honey," ran his fingers through his hair, stroked his back, and looked at him with what the patient called "cow's eyes."

Yet from the time he was 13 or 14, his parents and sister were preoccupied with what they interpreted as signs of his effeminacy. For example, they monitored such mannerisms as how he held a cup, telling him to not be and act like a "fag."

The closeness between himself and his sister had continued after his departure from her room. Their teasing, as they grew to adolescence, sustained its erotic quality. They would, for example, pull down each other's underwear in excited play. Each was possessive and jealous of the other. When her nose was put out of joint by his sixth-grade romance, his sister actively interfered and broke up the relationship. Yet she began to pull away, first in favor of girlfriend cliques and then dating. And it was then that he found a new twin, the classmate mentioned before. His sister and his mother continue to seem the most beautiful women he has ever met. In his sister's case this description was definitively refuted by serendipitous extraanalytic information. But the siblings' special intimacy ended with her marriage, a major, unthinkable disappointment and experienced infidelity that has changed their relationship irremediably.

DISCUSSION AND CONCLUSIONS

To summarize:

The patient felt himself derogated, intimidated, and deprived as a boy, and observed and identified with his father's inferior status. He was shown through his sister and the other women in the family that a girl was prized and enjoyed special relationships and satisfactions he was denied. To a disproportionate degree he identified hostilely with his mother. His father's seductive behavior and the family's nagging intimidations further compromised his sense of gender and identity. The constructive and structure-generating identifications with a father that are so important in a boy's individuation were instead replaced by conflict and pain. In short, the identifications that as internalizations are normatively indispensible in the structuralizations of development that include individuation as the cornerstone of identity were compromised. He was burdened from early on by the anxieties associated with the internal danger of his own rage over deprivation, derogation, rejection, and terrorization. His frightening, as well as unsupportive, environment further impeded individuation.

This review of the patient's life substantiates and further explains the diagnosis that he could not be a person with the capacities appropriate to his age and place in life, but instead sought an earlier intimacy, itself pathological, a twinning dating from early childhood. This was not, as proposed by Kohut (1971), fixation at a developmental phase apropos the primary object "in which not a primary identity but a likeness (similarity) with the object is established" (p. 122). It was much more and other than that, involving imitation and identification with a sibling, compromise formations involving need, aggression, and sexuality, a twinning reciprocity with the sibling, and defenses against profound anxiety. The fact of this identical twinship equivalent with a sibling of the opposite sex further compromised his own sense of gender, in addition to the factors enumerated in the preceding discussion and anamnesis. The patient entered adulthood too much an unformed child, not individuated, ignorant, unfulfilled, and conflicted about the very fundamentals of his sense of self and gender. He needed to be a part of two that could add up to one. While some of the material suggests incestuous and homosexual conflictual problems, it is the lack of a firm developmental substratum, a failure of individuation, that simultaneously predisposed to, shaped, and found expression in such issues. He remained an undifferentiated little boy, twinned to a little girl.

This case clearly demonstrates the place of individuation as an element in the genesis of intimacy. Because the patient was not a whole himself and was terrified by the anxieties involved in further progression, he could not participate in an appropriate gratifying and rewarding level of intimate experience. The consequence of this failure, consistent with Erikson's formulation, was isolation.

In this patient merger with another was critical in intimacy. But he did not conceive of merger as a psychological experience. It was for him a literal rather than symbolic union. So while he craved intimate satisfactions, both physical and psychological (between which he could not effectively discriminate), his terror of the experience of merger made it impossible for him to find intimate fulfillment except as a twin. This compromise formation between merging and being separate at the same time made any satisfactory resolution impossible. In being both he could be neither.

GENERALIZATIONS
AND QUESTIONS RAISED

The analytic authorities cited earlier presented merger between partners as the essence of the intimate experience. Does this case confirm that contention? Perhaps, but the threat of fusion as loss of self in someone who reacts to merger as if it were a physical reality rather than a phenomenon, the consequence of a psychological construction, does not demonstrate that the experience of intimacy at more advanced levels necessarily includes merger. On the one hand, the experience might be essentially the same but have a different impact in an individuated, structuralized, mental apparatus. The situation would then be one of regression in the service of the ego. But perhaps a more individuated personality, as part of more developed and organized capacities including symbolic functioning, would not experience or interpret adult intimacy as two becoming one in the same way.

The material demonstrates the importance of mutuality in intimacy, that is, both parties are believed to be involved by each. In this case, there was a requirement that the intimate partner and the intimate experiences themselves also be experienced as identical, consistent with a situationally defined twinship. But the mirroring required here may only be indicative of the needs at this level of psychological development and with this pathology. It is possible that with further individuation the sense that the experience is shared and has corresponding significance is its sine qua non.

With this patient the important element of exclusiveness, the exclusion of others from any form of intimate relationship with an involved subject, was clear. But, as with the issue of merger, it is difficult to estimate how much of this need for possession can, with maturation, be progressively played out in terms of a respect for, and appreciation of, each partner's uniqueness in relation to the other. For example, we expect mature parents to thrive in the atmosphere of different intimate experiences, involving others than themselves, within their family.

Basically, in these three areas of consideration, it is important to not fall prey to the prejudice that ultimate forms are simply recapitulations of the earlier experiences that underlie them, the so-called genetic fallacy. The answers to these questions are to be found in observational and clinical data rather than theory pushed beyond its reasonable applications.

Finally, infidelity was seen as a betrayal of intimacy. In this case it was clear that betrayal is assessed in the heart of the betrayed, rather than by conventionality or reason. Further, the participant's benchmarks of infidelity were in significant degree shaped by his limited degree of individuation as integral to his developmental status. Structuralization within the mind is very much the product of the accretion of identifications and internalizations that follow the inevitable losses of growth and life. When these disappointments and losses are construed as infidelities, compounded by the bitterness and rage of felt betrayal, individuation is retarded and skewed. When the disappointments and hurts of early phases are experienced as the products of infidelity, the ensuing rage-filled projective identifications and splitting buttress such paranoid positions. Then any frustration or loss may be forced into the procrustean bed of abandonment and disillusion. So, for victims of infidelity, real or imagined, the primitive power of regressive forces can be irresistible. How sobering it is to consider that in each of us may repose the incubus of an Othello or Medea. And yet the person described in this chapter did not have the potential to be an avenging angel. The involved structural issues transcended shattered self-esteem and loss of the other as another. After the initial shock, anger, and hurt of infidelity it was as if he were approaching a brand-new person in the form of his betrayer. No longer a function within himself, a she or he who completed his own persona, his former twin had lost meaning, and vengeance was irrelevant.

REFERENCES

Bettelheim, B. (1969). *The Children of the Dream.* Toronto: Macmillan.

Binstock, W. A. (1973). On the two forms of intimacy. *Journal of the American Psychoanalytic Association* 21:93–107.

The Compact Oxford English Dictionary (1991). New York: Oxford University Press.

Erikson, E. (1950). *Childhood and Society.* New York: W. W. Norton.

——— (1968). *Identity: Youth and Crisis.* New York: W. W. Norton.

Goldberg, A. (1989). *A Fresh Look at Psychoanalysis: The View from Self Psychology.* Hillsdale, NJ: Analytic Press.

Kohut, H. (1971). *The Analysis of the Self.* New York: International Universities Press.

Laplanche, J., and Pontalis, J. B. (1973). *The Language of Psychoanalysis.* New York: W. W. Norton.

Lichtenberg, J. (1991). What is a self object? *Psychoanalytic Dialogues* 1:455–479.

Mahler, M., Pine, F., and Bergman, A. (1975). *The Psychological Birth of the Human Infant.* New York: Basic Books.

Moore, B., and Fine, B. (1968). *A Glossary of Psychoanalytic Terms and Concepts,* 2nd ed. New York: American Psychoanalytic Association.

_____ (1990). *Psychoanalytic Terms and Concepts.* New Haven: Yale University Press.

Rycroft, C. (1968). *A Critical Dictionary of Psychoanalysis.* New York: Basic Books.

Stolorow, R. (1986). Critical reflections on the theory of self psychology: an inside view. *Psychoanalytic Inquiry* 6:387–402.

5

INSUFFICIENT INDIVIDUATION AND THE REPARATIVE FANTASY OF TWINSHIP

Discussion of Frank's Chapter "Intimacy and Individuation"

Helen C. Meyers, M.D.

Alvin Frank proposes that true intimacy cannot be achieved without a proper passage through the separation-individuation phase. He demonstrates this proposition with a clinical case whose subject is a patient unable to achieve intimacy due to a partial failure in individuation and core gender identity formation. Instead of true intimacy, this patient uses a pathologic compromise formation of psychological twinship. Frank's contribution is original, thoughtful, well written, and illustrated with beautiful clinical material. It appears deceptively simple but is really quite complex, touching on many important issues, such as the concept of intimacy and its development, the pathologic consequences of failure of individuation, and the use of psychological twinship. To my mind, Dr. Frank's chapter even attempts to make bedfellows of some concepts of Mahler's separation-individuation theory (Mahler and Furer 1968, Mahler et al. 1975) and Kohut's self psychology (Kohut 1971, 1977).

93

THE NATURE OF INTIMACY

Intimacy is a very important aspect of life and one well worth
analytic scrutiny. And while I do not think that intimacy is
what makes life sublime, I certainly believe that it makes life a
great deal richer. It is also important in psychoanalysis. Patients complain of the lack of intimacy in their lives and often
come to treatment for relief of this complaint and to become
able to experience intimacy. It is indeed often a goal in analytic
treatment to help the patient develop the capacity for intimacy. Yet I am not surprised that Frank could find few
references in the psychoanalytic literature on the topic of
intimacy. Because, strictly speaking, intimacy is an observable
interaction between two people, not a psychoanalytic concept. It is an interpersonal phenomenon, not an intrapsychic
one, although there are intrapsychic meanings, fantasies,
fears, and hopes attached to it. It involves an intersubjective
experience, an experience of closeness between two selves,
both mutually impacting on and changing the other.

There are, of course, many different definitions of intimacy. It involves a closeness between two separate individuals, a closeness that goes beyond ordinary friendship or
general object relationships. It does not involve concrete
merger (as it did for Frank's patient), nor does it necessarily
even involve general symbolic merger. The idea of such an
unconscious symbolic merger, the hope for and fear of it, is
related to a universal regressive pull to be reunited with
Mother, as pointed out by Chasseguet-Smirgel (1984) in her
conceptualization of the hope and fear in the oedipal period,
when the boy not only engages in and fears competition with
Father for Mother, but also has a fantasy of entering Mother's
womb and merging with Mother in intercourse, returning to
the earlier state of union with Mother—a symbiotic union
early in life and a concept of intimacy later. Intimacy involves
more a partial or even temporary symbolic merger or union, a

certain limited crossing of the boundaries while maintaining a separateness and an individual identity, somewhat akin to what Kernberg (1991) describes as the moment of orgasm in sexual union when there is a sort of crossing of boundaries and a momentary experience of the experience of the other.

Intimacy thus has certain qualities or conceptual aspects in common with empathy, although the latter is an intrapsychic concept. Erikson (1950) has described the development of the capacity for intimacy, assigning it to a particular time of life, that is, late adolescence, and involving the capacity for physical sexual intimacy with another, leaning on the physical experience of sexual intercourse, as well as the capacity for psychological intimacy following the development of identity formation. Failure in this achievement at this epigenetic critical point would lead to the opposite—that is, to isolation. Binstock (1973), as Frank points out, expanded the experience of intimacy to a second discrete period, or rather to an earlier specific period, the early mother–child relationship; both Erikson and Binstock stress the importance of the physical experience of closeness between mother and child in the early phase, and between sexual partners in late adolescence, as the important substrate for intimacy. Now, Binstock's extension might pose some conceptual problems, given that it involves not two complete individuals but one formed (the mother), the other still in a formative stage (the child). (This, again, echoes the concept of empathy. Strictly speaking, what we mean when we speak of empathy from the child toward Mother is responsiveness or identification; only the mother can temporarily identify while maintaining awareness of her own separateness and identity.)

Frank offers us a solution to this problem by postulating two different types of intimacy: one involving the mother and child that leads to the ability to separate and individuate, which he calls "formative intimacy," and the other—"capacity for intimacy"—based on individuation, selfhood, and a sense of self and identity, a capacity not reached in Frank's clinical case. Frank does not, as do Erikson (1950) and Binstock (1973), postulate one or two specific periods for the development of intimacy (nor does he stress the physical union, only the symbolic representation of psychological merger); rather, he postulates a developmental line with different intimacies along different stages and phases of development. I agree with Frank that there are many stages in the development of intimacy and that there are many different intimacies in adult life, such as between lovers, friends, family members, patient and analyst, and so on. What I miss in his discussion, despite his claim that a good deal has been written about these developmental stages in the literature, is some idea of his own developmental line for normal and pathological intimacy.

DEVELOPMENTAL BACKDROP

A successful separation-individuation process, the establishment of boundaries between self and object, and a sense of separate self and identity, are indeed prerequisites for the capacity for intimacy in the adult. These prerequisites are necessary for a sense of oneness with another—for any kind of partial symbolic merger or fusion—without the loss of self or concrete fear of loss of boundary and fusion manifested in Frank's patient. Here Kohut's (1971, 1977) critique of Mahler's separation-individuation constitutes a misunderstanding of Mahler's concepts. Kohut mistakenly suggests that the goal of separation-individuation is separateness and splendid isolation, and does not appear to appreciate that separateness and individuation are prerequisites for object relatedness, closeness, and intimacy.

Many of us (Akhtar 1994, Blum 1981, Burland 1986, Lax 1980, Mahler 1971, Mahler and Kaplan 1977) have worked on finding evidence in adult pathology for failures in the separation–individuation phase. This has, at times, been difficult, particularly to differentiate the problems of separation stemming from that period from separation issues relating to later phases in life, such as those relating to the oedipal period. However, much less work has been done specifically on the potential pathologic consequences of a failure of individuation in the separation–individuation period. Frank postulates a direct relationship between failure in intimacy later on and failure in individuation. In fact, he reasons that one of the potential pathological consequences of failure or partial failure in individuation may lead to an inability or lack of capacity for true intimacy later on.

Individuation involves content, the formation of a sense of self and identity, and is related to identification and internalization and mirroring. Separation involves boundaries between self and object, a sense of a separate self, and is related to such things as perception, motor development, speech, an ability to say no, and so on. But the various aspects of separation–individuation cannot be so easily separated out. For example, when Frank discusses his patient's equating intimacy with merger, he says that the patient feels both the loss of self-identity (i.e., individuation) and the loss of boundary between self and other, and probably loss of the other as well. Frank seems to equate individuation with identity in general. I do not. Full identity formation belongs in the later stages of adolescence as described by Erikson (1950, 1959), although Frank is right that certain aspects of identity are first formed in the process of individuation during the separation–individuation phase. Thus, as described by Stoller (1968), Kleeman (1966, 1976), Money and Ehrhardt (1972), and others, core gender identity, the awareness of oneself as male or female, is laid down during the second year of life by way of cognition, identification, and parental gender assignment, as well as certain hormonal aspects, while gender role

functioning is not consolidated until later, and sexual identity
and other aspects of identity are not consolidated until late
adolescence.

INCOMPLETE INDIVIDUATION AND
PSYCHOLOGICAL TWINSHIP

Frank postulates in his patient an inadequate and incomplete
individuation, particularly manifesting in a core gender confusion that interferes with his capacity for intimacy. Certainly, this interference in individuation is only partial, and
intrapsychic separation has been accomplished to the point
that the patient is able to have good general external object
relations, has many friends, and functions well in school and
at work. It is only with the possibility of intimacy with male
or female partners—which represents to him the threat of
physical merger or fusion, and a loss of a sense of self–identity
and boundaries—that the problem becomes obvious. To
Frank's patient, fusion or merger in this situation is not symbolic or partial but concrete and total. First, he does not quite
know whether he is a boy, a man, or a woman. This, according to Frank, is related to the patient's problem in im-
properly identifying with Father as a result of the family
constellation: a strong mother and a highly admired and
valued sister, together with a weak and devalued father. The
patient could not fully and satisfactorily identify with either
mother or father and thus could not definitely choose a
partner of either gender, fearfully running from intimacy with
either gender to the other. Second, the patient also probably
experienced some failure in development of symbolic thinking, a cognitive development that takes place between the ages
of 2 and 4, around the same time separation–individuation
takes place. The patient's flaw in symbolic thinking may not,
of course, be a total failure, since he seems to be functioning

well academically and in other areas where the ability for symbolic thinking is required. However, it may fail him under the pressure of intimacy.

Frank comes up with an original and fascinating formulation of how the patient attempts to solve this wish for, and dread of, intimacy by positing a search for a "twin" in this patient. In other words, he believes the patient came up with an ingenious solution or compromise formation of twinning, which to the patient is halfway between his wish and his fear, constituting a kind of safe intimacy, avoiding both the danger of concrete physical merger and the coldness and loneliness of isolation. This, according to Frank, is a pathologic, defensive, regressive solution that involves an unformed self that needs a twin to make a whole self. This is an enacted fantasy, the twin in the original developmental situation having been his sister who was both slightly younger and of the opposite gender, and the twin now sought being not a real twin but a psychological representation of a twin. For this patient the fantasy involves, among other things, exclusiveness and possessiveness, and any rupture of this exclusiveness means betrayal and infidelity, the patient reacting with withdrawal and painful rupture of the twinship intimacy. A vicious circle is set up, with immaturity leading to pathologic twinship, which readily gives way to a paranoid sense of betrayal that leads to withdrawal and a loss of sense of self, which, in turn, again leads to the seeking of twinship for completion.

A great deal has been written about both fraternal and identical twins (Arlow 1960, Burlingham 1946, 1949, Dibble and Cohen 1981, Glenn 1966, Joseph 1959). These writings, largely though not exclusively, refer to biologic twins from birth onward. The impact on the psychologic development of the child of being a twin has been discussed in terms of its supportive and problematic aspects—the intense competition as well as closeness—the twins' sense of incompleteness, their need for the other to make a whole, the simultaneousness and equivalence of their experience, as well as the impact on internal object relations, self and object representations, and on actual external object relationships. In Frank's patient the process is, of course, in the opposite direction. Thus, discussion of the effect of biological twinship on development does not seem quite relevant here, since the patient is using his fantasy about it for his own purposes. It is, however, intriguing how much the patient unconsciously uses actual twin experience in his unconscious fantasy, as if it had been his own real experience.

According to Frank, this fantasy is created by the patient in order to deal with and repair defective development, his incomplete individuation, and his need for an "other" to make him whole. This accounts for his need for the complete identity and equalness of both twins, in terms of exact sameness of feelings, experience, attitudes, object relations, and personality, his insistence on complete mutuality, not only in both partners' acceptance of the other as a twin, but in his insistence on the same experience of the relationship in both—all based on the earlier developmental interference in individuation. If the twinship is to repair, then any deviation from sameness or any inclusion or interest in another, a third person, would constitute a terrible threat to the reparative fantasy, a rupture leading to panic and rage, and angry sense of betrayal experienced as infidelity, as discussed above and described by Frank. (Infidelity in Frank's chapter is discussed only in terms of this patient's experiencing the other's breaking of the fantasized twinship and not in terms of the developmental aspects of actual infidelity. Of course, fear of intimacy may lead to defensive acting out in infidelity, or anger at and disappointment in perceived or anticipated betrayal of hoped for and fantasized twinship could lead to angry, revengeful, and "self-protective" enactment of infidelity on the part of the imagined injured party. What would determine the choice of defensive action—such as avoidant withdrawal from intimacy and turning to the other gender or angry retaliation by infidelity—is, of course, a whole other question related to different individual factors and developmental issues.)

Another question that arises is whether this twinning is a pathologic defensive compromise formation or an arrest in development. It is of interest here to note that it fits rather neatly into Kohut's (1971) description of the three stages of mirror transference based on three steps of normal development. The lowest level, or "merger transference," involves a sense of the nonexistence of the other except as merged with the self. The second, slightly higher level, the "twinship transference," involves a sense that the other is an exact twin of the patient with the same simultaneous feelings, wishes, and thoughts. The third or highest level, the "true mirror transference," involves the acknowledgment of the existence of the other, with different feelings and wishes, but these are not felt to be of any real importance. The only important aspects of the other are his self–other functions for the patient, that is, the mirroring, reflecting, and empathic response to the patient's wishes, needs, and thoughts. These transferences are, in Kohut's theory, related to corresponding developmental steps in which development can be arrested due to lack of empathic resonance from the primary objects.

The description by Frank of the twinning in his patient fits neatly into the middle or twinship level—the fantasy and need for the other to be, and feel, exactly like the patient to make the latter feel whole. Such twinship transference and use of the analyst could then explain the patient's improvement by "transmuting internalization" of the empathic analyst. It is also interesting to note that in Kohut's description of these three levels of mirror transferences, in the merger transference the other's (i.e., the analyst's) differences are not recognized as such; in the mirror transference proper the analyst's differences are of no importance; but in the twinship transference any difference or divergence manifested by the other, the analyst, is highly upsetting and unacceptable to the patient, and reacted to with fear, shock, and anger—as a kind of betrayal or "infidelity" on the part of the analyst. Of course, whether Kohut, with all his stress on lifelong selfobject functioning, is really talking about true intimacy as I have defined it, a special, close relationship with partial crossing of boundaries between two separate individuals, is an open question. Kohut talks about the other, the object, almost exclusively in terms of selfobject or selfobject function, that is, the use of the other for completion and cohesiveness of the self, not as a separate object. It is only more recently that some self psychologists, for example, the Shanes (1989), have talked about the "otherness" function within the self—that is, the function within the self that is involved in meeting the self needs of the other—as well as the selfobject function of the other meeting the needs of the self. Still, there is no real talk of separate people, which is why Kohut may have misinterpreted Mahler's separation–individuation process leading to isolation as a goal in itself rather than the goal being relatedness and the capacity for intimacy between two complete, separate, individuated persons.

AN ALTERNATE VIEW

To play the devil's advocate one could suggest alternative theoretical explanations for the patient's pathology in intimacy and gender confusion. One such dynamic formulation based on oedipal complex issues and castration anxiety might be the following: With an angry, cold, distant, domineering but attractive mother; an overvalued sister; and a weak, devalued father, the patient might wish to identify with the aggressor and deny his maleness and identify with the woman. At the same time, in the oedipal struggle the patient might fear castration not only from the competitive rival but also from his strong, rejecting mother, as well as increased guilt for his competition with the weak father, and thus fearfully and guiltily withdraw from interest in the woman (mother) and intimacy with her, and defensively turn to the man (father), particularly in view of the father's affectionate, seductive advances. However, the father's devalued status and apparent helplessness and weakness, his potential for oedipal castrating revenge, as well as the prerequisite castration involved in taking the role of the woman with the man might then turn the patient away again from commitment to intimacy with the man. This could explain his bouncing back and forth from interest in, and frightened withdrawal from, intimacy with men or women, as well as his confusion of self-experience of gender identity as man, woman, or boy. His self presentation of being "unformed" could then be viewed as defensive to hide his oedipal conflicts. All this could create the picture that the patient presents. His search for a close, twin-like friend could thus be seen as a need for support from another who would not threaten intimacy with a member of the opposite gender and yet partially also represent the opposite gender as well, and who would help avoid the loneliness of isolation. This is similar to the need for a relationship with a "buddy" in puberty, when the boy seeks another individual very similar to himself, with a penis, for support and reassurance against castration at a time when he cannot tolerate such closeness with a parent who would be threatening either as an oedipal rival or a forbidden incestuous object. A buddy relationship avoids dangerous competition with the other, in which one would have to be up and the other down. The exact equality between the buddies assures psychosomatic safety. This does not necessitate an assumption of a defect in the sense of self or incomplete separation–individuation. We are reminded, of course, of Freud who, according to his own account, always had a need for a "brother" or "twinlike" relationship based on early experience with his cousin that he repeated with Fliess, Ferenczi, and others. This, according to Freud, was based on oedipal factors, avoidance of competition, castration fears, and need for mutual support in dangerous self-assertion.

These are, of course, only speculations. I do not know enough about this patient to make any really applicable, meaningful clinical formulation. I must admit, however, that in actuality I infinitely prefer Frank's formulation.

REFERENCES

Akhtar, S. (1994). Object constancy and adult psychopathology. *International Journal of Psycho-Analysis* 75:441–455.

Arlow, J. (1960). Fantasy systems in twins. *Psychoanalytic Quarterly* 29:175–199.

Binstock, W. A. (1973). On the two forms of intimacy. *Journal of the American Psychoanalytic Association* 21:93–107.

Blum, H. (1981). Object inconstancy and paranoid conspiracy. *Journal of the American Psychoanalytic Association* 29:789–813.

Burland, J. A. (1986). The vicissitudes of maternal deprivation. In *Self and Object Constancy,* ed. R. Lax, S. Bach, and J. A. Burland, pp. 324–348. New York: Guilford Press.

Burlingham, D. T. (1946). Twins. *Psychoanalytic Study of the Child* 2:61–73. New York: International Universities Press.

———— (1949). The relation of twins to each other. *Psychoanalytic Study of the Child* 3/4:57–72. New York: International Universities Press.

Chasseguet-Smirgel, J. (1984). *Creativity and Perversion.* New York: W. W. Norton.

Dibble, E. D., and Cohen, D. J. (1981). Personality development in identical twins. *Psychoanalytic Study of the Child* 36:45–61. New Haven, CT: Yale University Press.

Erikson, E. (1950). *Childhood and Society.* New York: W. W. Norton.

———— (1959). *Identity and the Life Cycle.* New York: International Universities Press.

Glenn, J. (1966). Opposite-sex twins. *Journal of the American Psychoanalytic Association* 14:736–759.

Joseph, E. (1959). Unusual fantasy in a twin: inquiry into the nature of fantasy. *Psychoanalytic Quarterly* 28:189–206.

Kernberg, O. F. (1991). Sadomasochism, sexual excitement, and perversion. *Journal of the American Psychoanalytic Association* 39:333–362.

Kleeman, J. A. (1966). Genital self-discovery during a boy's second year: a follow up. *Psychoanalytic Study of the Child* 21:358–392. New York: International Universities Press.

———— (1976). Freud's view on early sexuality in the light of direct child observation. *Journal of the American Psychoanalytic Association* 24:3–27.

Kohut, H. (1971). *The Analysis of the Self.* New York: International Universities Press.

_____ (1977). *Restoration of the Self.* New York: International Universities Press.

Lax, R. (1980). The rotten core: a defect in the formation of the self during the rapprochement subphase. In *Rapprochement: The Critical Subphase of Separation-Individuation,* ed. R. Lax, S. Bach, and J. A. Burland, pp. 439–455. New York: Jason Aronson.

Mahler, M. (1971). A study of the separation–individuation process and its possible application to borderline phenomena in the psychoanalytic situation. *Psychoanalytic Study of the Child* 26:402–424. New Haven, CT: Yale University Press.

Mahler, M. S., and Furer, M. (1968). *On Human Symbiosis and the Vicissitudes of Individuation.* New York: International Universities Press.

Mahler, M. S., and Kaplan, L. (1977). Developmental aspects in the assessment of narcissistic and so-called borderline personalities. In *Borderline Personality Disorders: The Concept, the Syndrome, the Patient,* ed. P. Hartocollis, pp. 71–86. New York: International Universities Press.

Mahler, M. S., Pine, F., and Bergman, A. (1975). *The Psychological Birth of the Human Infant.* New York: Basic Books.

Money, J., and Ehrhardt, A. A. (1972). *Man and Woman, Boy and Girl.* Baltimore: Johns Hopkins Press.

Shane, M., and Shane, E. (1989). The struggle for otherhood: implications for adult development. *Psychoanalytic Inquiry* 9:466–481.

Stoller, R. (1968). *Sex and Gender.* New York: Science House.

6

MALE INFIDELITY IN LONG MARRIAGES: SECOND ADOLESCENCES AND FOURTH INDIVIDUATIONS

John M. Ross, Ph.D.

Like heredity, Margaret Mahler goes on.

In an era when postmodernist sentiments have penetrated psychoanalytic precincts, many clinicians are preoccupied with so-called intersubjectivity in the conjoint construction of personal narratives. They tend to disavow their roots in the developmental ego psychology of bygone days and its most creative proponents: Hartmann, Jacobson, Erikson, Blos, Winnicott, and, of course, Mahler. Inattentive to their own history, they further despair of reconstructing that of their patients, indeed, dismissing such an endeavor as a naive confounding of psychic reality and (to borrow from Erikson 1964) a personal and interpersonal historical actuality that is, they aver, beyond the ken of a psychoanalytic archeologist. Absorbed by the here-and-now transference, they forget that it was Mahler who most clearly articulated the vagaries of the very "intersubjectivity" that has become the hue and cry of the postmodern psychoanalyst but who also dared to tie this phenomenon to early ego and object-relational development. Indeed, our current cognizance of the complexity, ambiguity, and tenuousness of what is now referred to as the "subject"—variously labeled the self representation, the self, ego identity, ego in the past—is presaged in Mahler's and her co-workers' observational studies of separation-individuation (Mahler et al. 1975). The contemporary language may be different, but, unacknowledged, the Mahlerian influence goes on.

MARGARET MAHLER'S LEGACY

Mahler's ideas about the dawn of consciousness can illuminate later mental life. Her concepts also continue beyond toddlerhood, adumbrating aspects of the oedipal era, adolescence, and adulthood in which most of us spend most of our days on earth. As Blos (1974), Settlage (1988), Akhtar (1995), and others have remarked, some of the developmental or—as I prefer to call them when referring to postadolescent phenomena—adaptational processes described and conceptualized by the Mahler group shed light on the intrapsychic crises and what used to be called structural changes later in the life cycle, that is, for those of us who still believe that life history matters and who are less wary of universalizing in our theorizing (if not necessarily our practice) than many of our contemporaries.

To be sure, past applications in this vein have been open to legitimate critiques, critiques centering on their naive reductionism. As with Winnicott (1963)—so with Mahler—the preverbal mysteries of infancy and toddlerhood have a seductive appeal. Imbued with Mahlerian fervor, many careless adherents erred on the side of those notorious genetic fallacies to which we psychoanalysts so often fall prey. Some of them oversimplified the object-relational evolution inferred by Mahler from her wealth of behavioral observations and crudely equated these intrapsychic processes with interpersonal transactions. Heedless of Piaget's cautionaries about the irrevocability of development (1929), others assumed that an earlier ego state could be revived in its original form once it had been superseded by subsequent personality structuralization. Looking for them, they saw in their adult patients' regressions revivals and reenactments not merely of some adolescent or even rapprochement fantasy or illusion of symbiosis with mother but the actual "dual unity" as it was experienced before the dawn of representational thought, verbalization, and so on. Innocently, they claimed to be able to go back in time with developmentally arrested or regressed analysands and, in a variant of the corrective emotional experience, to fix what had gone wrong. Still others took it for granted that the objects or, to use Spitz's felicitous terms (1965), preobjects to which these processes—symbiosis, separation, and individuation—had relevance in later life stages must perforce remain the same as they were for the infant and toddler who were first subject to them. Failing to distinguish fact from fancy, to discriminate among ascending orders of inference, and to substantiate speculation or at least call it what it was—they saw preoedipal mothers and, later on, preoedipal fathers everywhere in the psychic life of their patients. And they did so even when the evidence suggested that they were dealing with representations of the many other real people crossing the paths of their patients' journeys through life: brothers and sisters, fathers and mothers of latency and adolescence, sons and daughters, husbands and wives, and so on.

Above all, they confounded the primal process of separation of self and object—which later infant researchers have gone on to deem an almost preexisting human condition (see Stern 1977) and which is, at the very least, fundamentally achieved quite early on—with the more dynamic and evolving striving for individuation. Like object constancy, as

Mahler noted, the individual's efforts to determine what is his or hers and what belongs to somebody else continues as a lifelong project and is never fully realized. In contrast to the separation of self and object representations, individuation is a more complex process of self-articulation and self-sufficiency. It evolves throughout life at different levels and within different spheres of the personality, ebbing and flowing in the face of conflict and crisis, recruiting new casts of characters to serve as significant objects and subjects for new identifications and ongoing identity formation.

It is to some of the later editions of individuation that Mahler's perspective (together with those of her contemporaries Erikson, Blos, and Hartmann) can be most usefully applied, I believe. It is these later individuations that make life interesting—challenging for most of us. And so it is to them, or rather to one of them, that I will turn my attention.

PREAMBLE

In this chapter I draw from the work of Mahler as it has been elaborated by Peter Blos in his description of adolescence as a second individuation (Blos 1985). In particular, I focus on his work on the son's need at the point that his adolescence comes to its conclusion to disidentify with his father in order to crystallize a more independent and internalized ego ideal (Ross 1994). I will refer to some of my own thoughts about the uses of love in late adolescence and youth in facilitating a young man's disengagement from his father's protective functions and moral edicts and the ethical transformation that he undergoes in crystallizing his own ego ideal. And I will stress the male lover's projection of an erstwhile paternal ideal and attendant critical functions, both originally associated with a father's injunctions, onto the image of his female beloved.

Against this backdrop, I will try to demonstrate the development over time of a paternal and superego transference on the part of a husband onto the person of his wife. Once the object of death-defying desire, a man's erstwhile lover can, over the course of a life together, gradually come to represent a moral authority and thus appear to demand the deference owed to early parental figures. Particularly after the death of a man's actual father, or sometimes in concert with the adolescence of his children, when a sense of loss both calls for rejuvenation and further presents the urgent possibility of alternative lifestyles and values, a man may be moved to find himself again by seeking a lover or mistress with whom he can both dally and identify.

On the surface, it may seem that he is fleeing his preoedipal mother's grip in the arms of his wife and finding in his mistress a more illicit and therefore more oedipal object to exhibit to, conquer, and satisfy his phallic narcissistic lust. And to a degree, this need for renewed separation figures is one important motive for an extramarital affair. But it doesn't tell the whole or even the basic truth, I believe. Indeed, a more careful clinical exploration of transferences to these men's wives often unearths not the maternal but rather the silent paternal transferences they entertain toward them, and their partners' roles as "uxor pater familias, uxor loco parentis." Having attempted and partly carved out third individuations in parenthood earlier on or perhaps in the sort of immigration phenomena described recently by Akhtar (1995), these husbands now plunge into last-ditch efforts, consciously defiant and even deliberately regressive, at "second adolescences" and "fourth individuations." However destructive may be the results or primitively misguided the whole enterprise at times, the agendas involved have a progressive impetus behind them—namely, some final stab at finding something new in a state of renewed abandon and at becoming even more of an individual, at finding out what they truly feel and thus believe.

A CLINICAL EXAMPLE:
THE AFFAIR IN HINDSIGHT

"What I wonder," mused Irv, aged 64, "is why I didn't leave Leah for Ann." A patient in a thrice-weekly psychotherapy with me, initially undertaken because of what he and his wife of forty-four years called his "manic" behavior, Irv Schoenfeld was recalling the love affair twelve years earlier whose aftermath had precipitated a first course of psychotherapy (with another analyst). When he had been in the throes of his passion for Ann, this "daughter of Venus" whose clitoral anatomy, he said, had made her capable of multiple orgasms and who shared the cultural interests scorned by his pretty but philistine wife, he hadn't had the slightest interest in the process of self-reflection.

He needed to cool down first and exercise hindsight. Irv Schoenfeld was and always fancied himself a doer. Mildly claustrophobic and "unable to slow down," he was a man who had defied deprivation and convention to extricate himself from the "ghetto" and what he called his "peasant parents" to become an internationally acclaimed scientist, academic, and foundation administrator. Yet now, slowed by the inevitability of aging and the renal disease that was at last making its effects felt, he was surprised by his thoughts. They were not what he had expected nor what his high-school sweetheart and lifetime companion would have wanted them to be.

What Irv was thinking was that his whole life, a life filled with adventure and discovery, Leah—so cold when it came to

Irv's doings apart from her (once breathtakingly beautiful, she was herself no slouch as a lover, at least when it came to sex)— had held back as if trying to hold him back. She never praised him—"God forbid!" He would bring her gifts from his trips, exotica from climes other than Great Neck, and she'd still not respond. He'd suggest that she listen to his beloved opera and read his cherished novels—to no avail. She'd be seductive with their son before his very eyes and then just disavow her behavior. She hated going to the functions that his work required and unequivocally refused to join in helping cele- brate his many honors and awards. Apart from sexual de- mands and indulgences, there were all those times, all those months and years when they "drifted like ships passing in the night." He got so little from her, so little intimacy and empa- thy, that now he wondered why he hadn't accepted Ann's celebratory welcome, extended when the children were gone yet Leah was still young and desirable enough to garner the lovers and the love that he felt she deserved. Perhaps it wouldn't have lasted, but for a while Irv would have had the soul mate for whom he'd always yearned. But he just couldn't, couldn't go the distance. "Something like guilt" drew him back, he opined, or maybe it was his jealousy when Leah retaliated with an affair of her own, with a rich lawyer like his brother Stanley. Whatever the pull back was, it was too powerful to resist. He had said good-bye to Ann finally, got sick with his first kidney infection, and—having moved out of his house briefly during the affair—moved back in with his wife, who nursed him through the illness. Leah, ignoring his healthy achievements, was always there for him when he got sick—always, just as his parents had been for Stan, frail from toddlerhood on. For Stan, that is, but never for him. They had taken Irv for granted, and taken it for granted that this other, older son could take care of himself.

Reflecting back on his long and complex life, freed by virtue of the passage of time from the conflicting erotic and moral imperatives that infuse a passionate affair in process, Irv Schoenfeld was able to contemplate the timorousness and deep dependency haunting his otherwise passionate and icon-oclastic life. He'd gotten so far in it. Yet just as he never deserted his parents and siblings when they were in need, he had always come home again—home to Leah, not just Leah and the children, but to Leah herself. He needed her. He was scared—scared to leave. And he was guilty—overcome by "something like a separation guilt," he added. For all his bravado, Irv was forever endangering or actually injuring himself, hobbling himself, returning outstretched, offering himself, his broken self, up to Leah's ministrations, to her admonitions, prostrate before her recriminations. And that was how he found himself "an analysand in spite of [him] self." And once more he'd followed his wife's near ultimatum of advice. Still, he wondered, why did he embrace her limited and unimaginative worldview, so much of which he found empty or downright objectionable?

They *had* lived a long life together. Irv and Leah, the middle-class girl whose house and family he had admired from afar at first, had met when he was 17, she 16. Irv was taking her home from about their fourth date, and they were riding in an elevator (and not climbing flights of dimly lit stairs to his family's ramshackle rooms)—an elevator up to her family's carpeted apartment on Pelham Parkway. Irv kissed her on the lips, hard and deep, and reached under her blouse into her bra, cupping the beautiful girl's young breast. Finding her nipple, he found himself exclaiming, "I love you—forever!" Forever.

Irv had found his way out. He had found his way away from the coarse first-generation parents who screamed at each other in Polish and Yiddish and ignored their son's emotional needs and intellectual sensitivities. He had escaped the mother and father who openly hated each other, the parents who failed to show up on time for their firstborn son's bar mitzvah because they were closing their store and making some last-minute money, the mother whom he consciously hated and the father whom, inexplicably, he had loved—not just purported to love his whole life but truly loved—even while he despised what he stood for. He'd bettered the parents whose illnesses and old age and travails with Irv's brother and emotionally troubled sisters he'd always attended to.

Within six years the young couple had a house and four children—the family life denied Irv in his childhood as a near castoff in a dirty tenement. Somehow, working his night job and scrimping on stipends from educational grants, having left pharmaceutical school for biochemistry over everybody's objections, he'd managed to pay for this home. Irv had managed to care for the people in it better than he'd ever seen anybody care for anybody else before. And dutiful husband that he was, he did it even when Leah never seemed grateful. He took care of her, made love to her, supported her career even when he felt that his wife never shared his joie de vivre and his infinite enthusiasms.

Beginning in his forties, no less than a quarter of a century into their marriage, shortly after his father died of bladder cancer, he did begin to betray her. Irv either understood or rationalized the half dozen peccadilloes before Ann as a response to and retaliation for Leah's less boldfaced betrayals of the heart. Besides, he hadn't had that many, he averred, further remarking on his abiding prudery—his not having masturbated as a teenager or, more recently, his not having allowed himself to lie back and get a blow job from his wife until his therapy with me gave him "permission simply to show [himself] and receive pleasure." But, restive and histrionic, he did have his dramatic affairs, all of them with compelling women. There was the Russian chemist at the UN conference, the Thai anthropologist with parrots and monkeys in her hotel room, the Italian diva, even the world-famous woman psychoanalyst—all of them lovers who gave his enthusiasm back to him in the form of their own, invigorating him with their love of him, of his accomplishments, and of life itself. But in the end he always came back to Leah. That is, until Ann posed the real threat, and Leah became depressed and then wild in her own right, and the children, who were now adults, blamed him entirely, and everyone said he should get help.

In point of fact, it had been pretty good for the last dozen monogamous years. No, they'd never come together over books, or opera, or chamber music. But they'd made love a lot, dealt with their squabbling and achieving children and grandchildren as they should, and fought a little bit about Irv's workaholism. And he still did have a way of running off to jungles, islands, and mountains and getting injured or ill, much to his more homebound wife's consternation. Then he had gotten really sick again with the old kidney problem, but only more ominous in an older man, and had acceded at last to Leah's demand that he slow down and seek psychotherapy again. He'd been surprised and increasingly intrigued—amid his grumbling reticence, his resistance to sitting still and relying on a man like me, and his bouts of seemingly macho but mostly masochistic acting out—by what he was finding out.

At first I saw my patient's affairs, apart from expressions of his zest for life, as efforts to escape the hold of his withholding wife, whose cool style might have been different but whose perceived compulsion to deprive him of any narcissistic satisfaction was like that of his strident mother. He was, I reckoned, forever trying to free himself from the unnurturing and emasculating arms of his preoedipal mother. Beset by separation guilt indeed, and by a fair share of remorse over more oedipally toned conquests, he would get himself hurt and return with his nearly severed tail between his legs, seeking solace and forgiveness at the price of masochistic surrender. Moreover, Irv's yearning for mothering seemed to be reflected in the transference and countertransference. Often struck by my patient's reckless endangerment of himself physically, I found myself moved to act as the overprotective Jewish mother he had had in life only after falling on his face. I thought about this dyad, about a perverse and protracted refueling, about the tensions of rapprochement, about Irv's lifelong disavowal of his undeniable dependency.

But this formulation didn't tell the whole story, not the story of Irv Schoenfeld's by then rather long and complex life. What, I asked myself, about the fact that, like other patients of mine who had succumbed to the charms of another woman in midlife, he had found Leah when he was so young and so unfinished. And what about the fact that he had used her as he had—again like other analysands—to get away from home— away, he said, from the "world of our fathers." And what about that resilient reaction formation, what about my patient's lifelong sentimentality when it came to that "undiluted sonofabitch father of mine"? It couldn't be that he was just too guilty to have a full-fledged oedipal victory, to go "too far beyond him."

It was only when Irv began to work on his memoirs, to "tell it like it is," to say to the world what his father was really like only when the dead man's spectral image floated like Hamlet's father into the bedroom and demanded his impotence while he was making love to Leah, that another layer of truth was exposed. It was then, in the midst of working through positive oedipal conflicts, that Irv recalled the bitterness and shame of having felt naked and invisible before a father, not mother, who never looked at him. In point of fact, Schoenfeld the elder had been more absent and withholding than his son's mother. He was a father who never noticed, much less cared for, his boy—a father who never knew what his son was studying, much less how spectacular his grades were; a father who never managed to see him play ball, much less hit one of his many home runs, bringing him "home but with nobody there." Irv may hardly have been the "docile shoe salesman type" who was further emasculated at home by the wife to whose authority he deferred (in fact like so many of the men in Leah's family). But he had nevertheless transposed his need for some ideal father and transfigured the image of one onto Leah's person and her initially more graceful world nearly a half century earlier. He had collected the few grains of hope she and her family offered in the way of a better life in order to forge an ideal, something to strive for yet to anchor and protect him. No matter that, like Freud's Fliess, Leah, the designated father figure, did not measure up to what he had made of her. Besides, because he needed to strive so hard and to remain an essentially good man, he'd never been able to accede to his mother's devaluation of or to his very own contempt for his father. He needed an illusion of decency and high-mindedness; he "needed an image to live up to." Divvying up his various internal objects and affects, Irv had made his father all good, his mother just as bad, further deflecting, in his recollections, his considerable filial violence onto his irresponsible siblings and the various other miscreants crossing his indignant path a he proceeded through life. Against all odds, he had wanted and contrived a beautiful, meaningful, manly existence.

But then the simple repetition won out. In time he substituted for his childhood squalor the banality and diffidence that he both found and provoked in his wife. Weighed down and empty, impatient with his neediness and reflexive dutifulness, Irv had felt compelled to break free if only for a while. He needed his intercourse with his fellow adventurers, women who extended their arms to him from the cultivated world he had greeted wide-eyed as a young man with the promise of intoxication and aspiration. It scared him, however, this betrayal not only of his wife but of his father—of his roots in the past that consciously he scorned. And so rather than get carried away into a brave new world, he had returned repeatedly to pay his homage and seek safety. Rebel that he was, fiercely independent and high-minded in the world of work and community, Irv Schoenfeld infallibly returned to the wife who didn't understand him, and in her guise to the father who had never even tried.

"Wherever I go," Irv noted, "whatever I think about, for sixty-four years—he's always there. I've always looked for a passionate love affair with an older man—my father, I see now. I didn't even have what little Shlomo [a boy Irv had taught in a yeshiva] had. His father beat him when he did my newspaper assignment. My father didn't care enough to do that. He did beat me—but only because I bothered him. I made Leah my father, or my ideal father, but she could be just as diffident as he. She could make me feel like that naked little boy, a plucked chicken waiting to have its kidneys cut, a little boy kicked helpless out of my room to make way for my brother. Only with Leah it was our son. I don't like to admit it—you're about my son's age, after all—but when I run away from you, it's that you are a father for me. I've run from them my whole life. But I cling to Leah. He's always there, my father—isn't he?"

In the context of this retrospection and after forgetting a session with me, the patient reported a dream:

"I'm swimming in the cold water with somebody clinging to my back. Then he's not there. . . . I swim on and get out on an iceberg. It's slippery, and I'm afraid to fall and hurt myself." Associating to it, he was reminded of his father's being a strong swimmer and of his clinging to his back, in one of their rare moments of closeness, on outings at Jones Beach. In the dream, he noted, he reversed this, making himself the one to depend on—much as he had done in his real life. Now he was afraid of depending on me. "Iceberg" reminded him of his erstwhile lover Ann, whose last name had been Berger, and the "slippery slope" of an extramarital affair. Not that it mattered, he averred, since he had always felt "left out in the cold."

While thinking about these longings and identifications, Irv Schoenfeld had a rare and agonizing bout of constipation, forcing him to miss one of his sessions. I was able to exploit this undeniably psychosomatic event and to interpret his underlying wish to be penetrated violently and sexually by his father and now by me. Missing his session, he had fled from these problematic desires. Picking up on this intervention with uncharacteristic openness, my patient proceeded to elaborate on his increasingly conscious longing for abuse rather than indifference from his father as the only form of passion, of "love," he could get from him. Thus, he was able to verbalize his organizing but hitherto unconscious fantasy of masochistic and homoerotic submission to the parent of the same sex, a fantasy that underlay his rationalized compulsion to punish, hurt, and incapacitate himself and to seek out violation. This was particularly poignant at the moment, as he contemplated the possibility of dialysis.

Serving abiding preoedipal needs, oedipal in origin and recast with the advent of adolescent genitality, such fantasies, I have found, lie at the core of neurotic conflict in general and, specifically, the tendency to surrender to a sadistic superego that is so characteristic of moral masochism. In other words, behind unconscious guilt and the neurotic deference to the moral masochist's critical conscience is the sexual, feminine masochism of which Freud wrote in his paper on the subject (1924). This harsher inclination complements a man's more gentle libidinal clinging to his paternalistic ideal, one that pertains to the ego ideal and is suffused more with libido than with aggression, more with love than with hate. On this note, I will return to the impact of the ego ideal and related paternal transference phenomena in later life.

DISCUSSION

Culling from my practice and those of my supervisees, I have chosen my clinical illustration to prove a point. I myself have treated four other men who have engaged in adulterous affairs approximately twenty years into their marriages, three in analysis and one other in psychotherapy. Three were in the throes of their infidelities at the time of treatment. One, like Irv, was older and was looking back on the experience from the vantage of hindsight. Partly for reasons of confidentiality, I have chosen as my example a man no longer under the sway of illicit passion and attendant conflict.

Notwithstanding differences in their ages, subcultural backgrounds, early development, and other circumstances, these men have certain features in common. In contrast to essentially narcissistic characters, for whom philandering is almost a way of life, my patients, who were not without their vanities and lapses, had nonetheless mostly erred on the side of moral masochism in their lifelong unwanted submission to sadistic and indeed narcissistic fathers, objects acting as unconscious superego agents. For reasons that may not be so clear, they all made lifelong commitments to teenage sweethearts. For reasons that are more evident, they eventually betrayed them, driven to do so in the face of powerful feelings of guilt and dread. In these dramas, in their unwanted love affairs, wives and lovers were cast as actors portraying some unlikely characters from the depths of the unconscious, characters hitherto interred in the structures of the mind. Let me elaborate.

More clearly than any other theorist, Peter Blos has developed Mahler's concept of individuation. In his paper "The Genealogy of the Ego Ideal" (1974) and volumes *On Adolescence* (1962) and *Son and Father* (1985), Blos has shown how the last psychic structure to crystallize, the individual's more or less autonomous "ego ideal," is internalized in a process that he terms "the second individuation." In particular, a young man must replace his tender, dependent, and perforce submissive tie to his cherished, protective, rescuer father with his own set of ideals, injunctions, and increasingly less self-serving value system. With adolescence, continues Edith Jacobson (1964), another of Margaret Mahler's theoretic collaborators and personal intimates (her third analyst), the ego ideal becomes disengaged from the primitive and ever more anachronistic superego system and further associated with the individual's ego functioning. In Erikson's (1963) less metapsychological terms, the postadolescent, having negotiated his identity crisis, replaces the morality of childhood with the ethics of the adult. He has become less governed by categorical imperatives and more capable of considered and responsible choice.

What I would further stress is that the ego ideal, so critical in maintaining a sense of self-esteem and of identity and so late in crystallizing, remains vulnerable to regression and open to choice throughout postdevelopmental adult life. It is in the sphere of aspirations, goals, and values and under the sway of environmental/adaptational pressures rather than of maturation and its developmental determinants, that further individuation can take place. Thus, so-called adult developmentalists and students of parental dynamics have underscored the possibility of a third individuation as a potential response to the emotional challenges posed by adult milestones and stressors. As I have noted, Akhtar (1995) describes the immigrant's internal upheaval in exactly these terms.

However, since the impetus for such changes is not biological in nature, they are by no means as inevitable as the by-products of development proper. One does not have to become a parent at all. A father can avoid and almost scotomatize his children. An immigrant can cling to his or her traditional ways and isolate himself or herself from the new cultural context. In adult life, an inevitable sequencing of phases does not exist.

Yet another caveat is in order when thinking about the nature of psychic change in adulthood. Whatever its elasticity, it is not the core self representation that is being reorganized but rather the more variegated and permeable layer of self closer and more responsive to the social surround. The ego ideal, along with the self-esteem and sense of ego identity achieved in its felt actualization and social affirmation, is more dynamically affected and volatile in adult life than its primordial form laid down in infancy and toddlerhood.

In order to clarify these processes, let me return to the late adolescent process and to my own further thoughts about how this Blosian transformation may best come to fruition. In earlier contributions on the developmental uses of romantic love in a man's late adolescence and young adulthood, I argued that such passion makes for an age-specific moral revolution (see Ross 1994). In its throes, the young lover defies paternal edicts to immerse himself in an erotic union that both revives preoedipal and oedipal transferences and transgressions of gender and generational boundaries and further confronts him with an altogether novel genital experience with a new and unique person. In its grip he finds, often to his dismay, that a good lover cannot remain a good son. Partly regressed, driven by impulse and ruled by feeling, more fluid in his boundaries, and dwelling in metaphors that contradict common sense, a young man comes to identify with his female beloved's femininity—including her interpersonal embeddedness, her emphasis on empathy, and her ethic of care, to borrow from Chodorow (1974) and Gilligan (1982). As a consequence of this introjective identification, he can then modify his sometimes strident adherence to principles of justice at all costs, abstractions that are derived from an underlying negative oedipal and masochistic submission in the face of the paternal castration threat. He can temper these absolutes with a more feminine and pragmatic voice of conscience. Thus, first love serves to gentle the youth's harsh critical conscience and to alter incompletely internalized ideals, whose covert agenda has been to please his father and, in emulating what he believes to be him, to win his male parent's proverbially conditional love. Less stereotypically masculine in his values and feelings, the young man who has loved (even if he has lost) has detached himself to some degree from childhood obeisances. He has become more of his own man.

Would that life were so simple and straightforward. Introjective identifications are interdependent with projective ones. Progressions are forever being undermined by the forces of regression and of neurotic inhibition and consequent entropy. Men seem to need their authority figures and their consequent moral masochism and remain abidingly uncomfortable with the freedom and solitude that are associated with autonomy. In spite of themselves, they crave their moorings and the illusions of protection and rescue these provide. Adults cling to the anachronistic superegos so necessary to early development but often so maladaptive in adult life. They hold on to moral superstition even while living in a world that they could govern far better with simple "insight and responsibility"—with the judgment and the discretion of an independent and thinking grown-up. They need to see themselves as little children in a world of omnipotent if also often cruel and depriving caretakers.

That is why we have religion, I suppose. That is why our patients have the transference readiness that we clinicians bank on in the first place in order to seduce them to stay with us (thereafter luring them into their increasingly lonely and exhilarating voyages toward personal discovery and emancipation). And that's why passion cools. That's why marriage becomes less a passionate choice than an obligatory institution. Let me elaborate again.

Over time in many if not most marriages, in subtle and

layered ways, a man returns to his father. His lover's power to wrest him from his preexisting condition (his surrender to the father of what Blos calls "the negative complex") has resided, in part, in his paternal and moral narcissistic transferences to her. And it is this projection that can win out once more over novelty and truth. Fearful of endless love with his lover so close at hand, a man reorganizes himself and seeks the psychic equilibrium he needs, he senses, to function in the real world as a provider. He does so by transforming his wife into a father figure who demands duty and performance and imposes her notions and values on his ways of thinking about himself and of conducting his family life. In the process, in yielding to such projected paternal constraints, emotional and erotic intensities are diminished, and the world around the lovers loses some of its luster and the illusory flowing quality it and they have had in the past. Ego boundaries and the reality principle are reestablished in a process analogous to the more primal one described by Loewald in 1951 in his paper "Ego and Reality."

Contrasting the alliance of marriage and the partnership of parenthood with the rash, impetuous, and narcissistic states of infatuation and of falling in love, many analysts refer to the more sober friendship of the couple as mature love. In so doing, stressing certain apparently adaptive features, they miss its regressive undertones and neurotic implications. What this gradual turn of events usually signals is an aim-inhibited, homoerotic, and self-denying submission once more to the overpowering agency of the same-sexed parent—with all the dependency; sexual, feminine, and moral masochism; and self-abnegation that go along with any inhibition of initiative, purpose, and vision.

Such transference phenomena are never simple matters, especially when they crisscross the lines of gender expectations. Impressed by a male patient's description of the wife who looms so large in his life, one is often tempted to see him as a little boy with a big, controlling, castrating mother. In so doing, the analyst often fails to pick up on the specific qualities and injunctions attributed to her by his patient. Conversely, representations of fathers as demanding if also ultimately benevolent despots derive in part from a son's erstwhile preoedipal maternal transferences to the father and father figures in his life. Without challenging directly his need to escape his mother's hold and to disidentify from her, and pointing the way instead toward masculine and independent achievement, these icons and their refractions within the superego can serve, as I have said elsewhere, as beacons of a disguised and surreptitious anaclitic reassurance. Doing well, performing well for a nearly implacable father may thus represent a way of returning to the womb of infancy, of becoming once again a babe in arms—the arms of the preoedipal mother. "Being a good husband" may take on these paradoxical meanings, thereby compromising a wife's status as an adult sexual woman.

Unable to see her as the person she is, a husband may be driven to seek erotic freedom elsewhere. And thus it is that the troubadours and courtiers of Aquitaine could declare that true romantic love was unimaginable within the domestic confines of marriage. Unrequited love, first love, adulterous love, they and other love theorists proclaimed, are the only true loves. Passionate truth requires the specter of the illicit, of obstacles to be overcome, of emotional danger. Ecstasy, they say, means being outside one's state in the world, jarred loose from normal consciousness and the narcissistic sheath of everyday existence.

Psychoanalysis has always had difficulty both conceptualizing and countenancing this typical state of affairs. Abrogating intimacy and inevitably entailing cruelty toward the wife of the adulterer (and toward his mistress as well), infidelities run counter to the prevailing psychoanalytic ethic and thus our assertions about what is normal, healthy, or adaptive in life. But then they are no less problematic for the men themselves—for men such as the Irv Schoenfelds of the world, hardly casual philanderers but, quite the contrary, scrupulous men whose more selfish impulses are at odds with their morality and whose lusty wives do not stint when it comes to slaking their obvious desires.

In these men, some greater force, overriding their compunctions and subsuming their various drive derivatives, propels them to complicate their lives—to close off important connections, abrogate certain intimacies for the sake of others, expand their boundaries, add to their identifications, be bad for a while, reorganize and reconstitute their sense of individuality. Something moves them to act and, following suit, to feel like teenagers once again, but teenagers equipped with the sexual savvy of a more middle-aged man. Something drives them toward second adolescences and fourth individuations.

The ideal would have it that these men free their images of their wives from outmoded and unwanted paternal and maternal transferences and, in so doing, free themselves in all spheres from the need to submit to authorities of their own making. This essentially oedipal effort might dislocate them interpersonally, and this adaptational revolution might result in extramarital affairs. Or, sometimes, a good and passionate marriage can survive this upheaval and thrive unperturbed. But most husbands as well their wives are not so mature and imaginative that they can contain all passionate possibilities within what has become their shared and enveloped psychic actuality over a whole lifetime together.

A CAVEAT IN CONCLUSION

We developmentally minded analysts must be more retrained, we are told by current critics, and watch out for irresponsible and potentially oppressive and discriminatory generalizations. Here I have tried to distill an impression based on a number of cases of the driving force toward further individuation that can motivate adultery in moral men after many years of marriage. To reiterate: the five cases that I happen to have treated have at least one important feature in common. To repeat: all these patients had married in late adolescence. How much their infidelities or the meaning attributed to them are artifacts of this late developmental variable remains to be determined.

REFERENCES

Akhtar, S. (1995). A third individuation: immigration, identity, and the psychoanalytic process. *Journal of the American Psychoanalytic Association* 43:1051–1084.

Blos, P. (1962). *On Adolescence.* New York: Free Press.

———— (1974). The genealogy of the ego ideal. *Psychoanalytic Study of the Child* 29:43–99. New Haven, CT: Yale University Press.

———— (1985). *Son and Father.* New York: Free Press.

Chodorow, N. (1974). Family structure and feminine personality. In *Woman, Culture, and Society,* ed. M. Z. Rosaldo and L. Lamphere. Stanford: Stanford University Press.

Colarusso, C. (1990). The third individuation: the effect of biological parenthood on separation–individuation processes in adulthood. *Psychoanalytic Study of the Child* 45:170–194. New Haven, CT: Yale University Press.

Erikson, E. (1963). *Childhood and Society.* New York: W. W. Norton.

———— (1964). *Insight and Responsibility.* New York: W. W. Norton.

Freud, S. (1924). The economic problem of masochism. *Standard Edition* 19:157–170.

Gilligan, C. (1982). *In a Different Voice: Psychological Theory and Women's Development.* Cambridge: Harvard University Press.

Jacobson, E. (1964). *The Self and the Object World.* New York: International Universities Press.

Loewald, H. (1951). Ego and reality. *International Journal of Psycho-Analysis* 32:10–18.

Mahler, M. S., Pine, F., and Bergman, A. (1975). *The Psychological Birth of the Human Infant.* New York: Basic Books.

Piaget, J. (1929). *The Child's Conception of the World.* New York: Harcourt, Brace.

Ross, J. (1994). *What Men Want.* Cambridge: Harvard University Press.

Settlage, C. F., Curtis, J., Lozoff, M., et al. (1988). Conceptualizing adult development. *Journal of the American Psychoanalytic Association* 36:347–370.

Spitz, R. A. (1965). *The First Year of Life.* New York: International Universities Press.

Stern D. (1977). *The First Relationship: Infant and Mother.* Cambridge: Harvard University Press.

Winnicott, D. W. (1963). *The Maturational Processes and the Facilitating Environment.* New York: International Universities Press.

7

EGOCENTRICITY AND INFIDELITY

Discussion of Ross's Chapter "Male Infidelity in Long Marriages: Second Adolescences and Fourth Individuations"

Lawrence D. Blum, M.D.

John Ross begins his chapter with an excellent, concise summary and critique of recent trends in psychoanalytic theory. It soon moves to the first of the main ideas and its central focus: men's paternal transferences to their wives. This is a very interesting, thought-provoking idea that I do not recall seeing or hearing elsewhere, and we should consider it carefully. The second main idea, the proposed fourth individuation, follows from these transferences. It is explained as an attempt to grapple with and seek a further degree of individuation, of psychological independence, from the restrictive paternal transference figure. Again, this is a novel and interesting idea although a bit further from the clinical data and at a higher level of abstraction; correspondingly, I find myself somewhat more skeptical.

MEN'S PATERNAL TRANSFERENCE TO THEIR WIVES

Let us first consider men's paternal transference to their wives. Ross's vignette about Irv Schoenfeld presents a significant amount of material in the patient's own words, and the material supports very nicely Ross's contention that this man had a substantial paternal transference to his wife, as well as, of course, a variety of other transferences and dynamics. Ross had made an astute clinical observation. What might this observation mean? What questions will test its mettle?

Despite the emphasis on the paternal transference, Ross explicitly recognizes the maternal transference, co-existing and distinct from paternal transference, and the preoedipal maternal transferences that developmentally prefigure the oedipal paternal transference itself. In fact, in his previous writings about men's difficulties in relationships with women, Ross has emphasized not their struggles with paternal transferences but their conflicts about their own maternal and feminine identifications, which are brought to the fore in the close company of women (Ross 1992).

So how much of the apparent paternal transference is actually paternal? Ross mentions early in his chapter that the paternal transference is also a superego projection of the patient. As a superego projection it obviously has very substantial paternal influence, but it has numerous other elements as well. Ross emphasizes the restrictive, denying, punitive aspects of this transference. His attributing it to the father is consistent with the reported data from the patient, with our knowledge of castration anxiety and the Oedipus complex, and, of course, also with Freud's theory of the superego (e.g., Freud 1923). But if the salient transference of this man to his wife is of a superego projection, we cannot assume the influence to be entirely paternal. Just as one thinks of developmentally earlier influences on the paternal transference, in parallel fashion one must also be mindful of early superego influences on later superego. As we have learned in previous Mahler symposia (e.g., Blum and Blum 1990), many early noes came from mother (or other early caregiver): Don't bite the nipple, don't throw food, don't play with the electric socket, and so on. The superego may be the heir to the Oedipus complex, but much of the inheritance was amassed earlier. And some of it later: we must be aware of postoedipal influences as well. Ross notes, following Blos (1967), the important revisions of superego and ego ideal in adolescence, which again have both paternal and nonpaternal contributions. (A part of the answer to Ross's question about the relationship between his male patients' late marital infidelities and their early marriages no doubt relates, as he implicitly suggests, to marriage before the second individuation process is sufficiently complete.)

While recognizing the paternal transference in its own right, we can also understand a variety of nonpaternal elements in it. Similarly, there is clearly a great deal of overlap between the paternal transference and the superego projection, but it is worth recalling that the two are not one and the same. It should be useful clinically to be able to oscillate between these two conceptual viewpoints. There is certainly more novelty in thinking about the paternal transference. We should "try it on," so to speak, and have it in mind as we listen to our patients.

While on the subject of this paternal transference, and before moving ahead to the topic of the fourth individuation, I would like to take a brief detour to note some other directions toward which Ross seems to me to be pointing. The first of these is the broader question of types of transference in marriages. We are accustomed to thinking of men's maternal transferences to their wives. And we are accustomed to thinking as a matter of course of women's paternal and maternal transferences to their husbands. Yet the notion of men's paternal transference to their wives seem new. Why don't we think of it? Is it present and we don't notice it? Is it often absent? We tend to look for a maternal transference in any dyadic relationship, and the possibility of a woman's paternal transference to her husband is obvious. With men, we usually think of father transferences to a figure apart from the wife, as part of a triad. Also, as Ross notes in his chapter, there is the matter of distinguishing between submission to the preoedipal or oedipal mother on the one hand and the preoedipal and negative oedipal submission to the father on the other. A further question now arises: When a man marries a "phallic woman," is his wife a disciplinary mother-with-a-penis, as has usually been assumed, or does the image contain an amalgam of a father transference? Again, Ross's idea expands our views of the potential transference situation within marriages.

The second area to which this observation (men's paternal transference to their wives) obviously extends is our thinking about therapy. Our literature has a growing number of articles about how the sex of the therapist influences the transference manifestations of the analytic or psychotherapy patient (e.g., Appelbaum and Diamond 1993). If all types of transference emerge in the marital dyad, irrespective of the partner's sex, this observation bolsters the traditional wisdom that the full range of transferences can arise within the analytic dyad, regardless of the sex of the therapist.

The case material Ross presents also bears on two other areas of ferment in our field: the boundaries between psychotherapy and psychoanalysis, and the role of the patient's age in treatment. While the patient is in thrice-weekly face-to-face psychotherapy, clearly a great deal of psychoanalytic work is accomplished, as suggested, for example, by analysis in the transference of some of the patient's conflicts over negative oedipal, homosexual submission. Additionally, the patient is in treatment at age 64, an age at which such analytic achievements used to be thought highly improbable. So Ross's case is of some import beyond the purposes for which it is intended in his chapter.

THE CONCEPT OF A FOURTH
INDIVIDUATION

Having concluded the detour, I would like to turn now to the idea of a fourth individuation. We are all familiar with the infantile separation–individuation process described by Mahler and with the second individuation of adolescence described by Blos. Now we are told that a third individuation may occur in conjunction with parenthood or in relation to immigration (Akhtar 1995). Oldham (1989), writing about development in middle age, has suggested that a third individuation process may occur when an individual's parents become older, need taking care of, and parent–child roles become reversed. Ross suggests a fourth individuation. A proper skeptic must ask, "What about a fifth or a sixth?" Skeptical or not, I think we would have general agreement that a degree of continuing individuation, of further differentiation between self and one's primary objects, can be a lifelong process, one that may be accelerated in a variety of compelling life circumstances.

Do we in fact have data to suggest that Ross's patient is actually undergoing a process of individuation? It is abundantly clear that Ross's patient is intensely conflicted. On the one hand, he is dedicated to negative oedipal submission to his father, to injury and punishment. On the other, he wishes to adventure, to achieve, to seek success and happiness. Clearly, he vacillates between these two poles. (There are, of course, numerous other conflicting dynamics as well, for instance, those relating to compliance and defiance, dependence and independence, and so on, but these may not be quite as central to the paternal transference.) Ross notes that his patient's infidelities are repetitions, and it seems to me that the evidence for this is just as compelling as the evidence that they are the developmental accomplishments of an individuation process.

As Ross notes, when Irv Schoenfeld met his wife, he was eager to leave the restrictive and neglectful world of his parents for the warmer and more well-to-do world of his wife and her family, and this is very much the same constellation that he experiences later in his excursions away from his wife into the seductive worlds of his other women. The only clear change is the position he attributes to his wife. There is a vacillation, a siding with first one facet of his conflict and then with the other, a darting away and returning, but is there actually a developmental process? We are accustomed with any neurotic symptom or conflict to find in it an attempt at a solution as well as an embodiment of conflict and regression, and I'm sure Ross is right in suggesting that this may sometimes be the case with infidelity. But does the idea of a fourth individuation provide, potentially, too easy a rationalization for infidelity as a possible developmental advance, as opposed to an expression of neurotic conflict?

Sometimes difficulties in marriages occur when one partner develops and outgrows initial neurotic inhibitions or conflicts and the other does not. This is one reason why analysis can sometimes lead to the weakening, rather than the strengthening, of a marriage. But often one indirectly observes the spouse of a patient change in the course of a patient's treatment as he or she accommodates to the patient. As the patient improves, and needs less to suffer, he more vigorously demands and often receives from his spouse more mature, or warmer, or less sadistic treatment, and so on, as the case may be. How much was Irv Schoenfeld engaged in a developmental process? How vigorous were his attempts to have his wife grow along with him? Or how much did he simply continue to repeat his earlier neurotic patterns? The point at which it sounds that Ross's patient *does* engage in a process that might approximate what we understand by the term *individuation* is when he is in treatment with Ross. At this point he starts to understand some of his conflicts and early identifications and can then start to resolve the conflicts and lessen the intensity of his relationships with his childhood parental images.

Ross is concerned with instances in which the marriage has become stale and passionless and erotic pursuits have been diverted from the marriage: it is these situations that lead him to his thoughts about paternal transferences and individuation. But what about marriages with different trajectories? For example, one sometimes sees in treatment people who seem well suited to their partners but for whom the early part of marriage is impeded by a great deal of neurotic conflict on the part of one or both partners. Often with experience and time, and sometimes with therapy or analysis, much better adjustment is achieved and the marriage becomes much more passionate than it was initially. The concepts of paternal transference or later individuations in marriages would have substantial utility if they prove to be pertinent across a broader spectrum of marriages, beyond the type that prompted Ross to the ideas he presents in his chapter.

THE ISSUE OF EGOCENTRISM

I'd like now to turn to another perspective from which to view this topic and this case. This is the matter of persistent human narcissism and egocentrism. Mahler described the differentiation process from the child's state of psychological symbiosis with Mother to that of a separate, individual self. As part of this process, the child experiences a gradually increased recognition of the mother (or other) as a separate object with her own needs. This awareness represents an enduring challenge to the egocentricity of the developing person. Just as Mahler named the last phase of separation-individuation "on the road to self and object constancy," that is, something never fully complete, the ability to set aside one's own omnipotence and self-importance and give others their full due remains likewise somewhat tenuous and seldom fully complete. We often see patients who are deeply dedicated to serving others, but always underneath there is a powerful, hidden *I want, I deserve, I need.* There is nothing new in this. We are particularly accustomed to observing these dynamics in instances of personality disorders and gross narcissistic disturbances. It is my impression, however, that we tend to overlook these features in cases we classify as "neurotic" or "oedipal."

This may be the case with theory as well as with clinical practice. A review of several of our commonly used texts finds that most of the discussions of the Oedipus complex emphasize the differences from the preceding phases of development rather than the continuities. Brenner (1973), Gabbard (1994), and Meissner (1985) all mention the shift from a dyadic "mother-and-child frame of reference" (Gabbard, p. 35) to a triadic one. Meissner, following Freud, describes a change from autoerotic to object-oriented libidinal interests. All three authors note the oedipal child's wish for exclusive possession of the opposite-sex parent and rivalry with the same-sex parent. Brenner, to his credit, takes pains to convey the deep passion of the child's oedipal strivings. What these authors do not note, and what I would like to add, is that the oedipal wishes are elaborations of earlier egocentric wishes for exclusive possession of the parent—and to be the apple of her (or his) eye. Similarly, oedipal rivalry and hostility follow from earlier anger at the frustration of these wishes.

The tendency to emphasize the developmental discontinuity (between preoedipal and oedipal phases) derives no doubt from our inclination to think in dichotomies, perhaps especially for heuristic purposes. It may also have origins in confusion about the term *narcissism*. Pulver (1970) has described the numerous meanings as well as problems following from its definition in terms of psychic energy. Narcissism, in energic terms, refers to self-directed libidinal investment. But analysts also have usually used the term *narcissistic* to indicate the meaning "egocentric." Oedipal strivings, by definition object directed, are not narcissistic in energic terms, and by linguistic confusion may be considered as not being egocentric. The child's egocentricity then ends with the onset of the oedipal phase. (For the sake of clarity here, I have generally endeavored to use the more specific *egocentric* rather than the more ambiguous *narcissistic*.)

Thus, a semantic and theoretical problem may have contributed to a tendency to underemphasize the essential egocentrism, the fantastic chutzpah, of the child's oedipal wishes. Our theories of development stress the difficulties that arise as the child enters the oedipal phase not yet having satisfactorily integrated good and bad object representations or sufficiently differentiated self from other. But even in auspicious circumstances, with the establishment of satisfactory self and object representations, the child leaves the preoedipal phase very preoccupied with issues of his relative size and relative importance, and he is still intensely, humanly wishful. If this were not the case, we wouldn't have an Oedipus complex in the first place: oedipal wishes are almost by definition self-centered. Just as oedipal wishes are renounced only partially and with difficulty, so is the child's normal egocentrism that motives them. I believe that analysis of the egocentric and other narcissistic features of neurotic patients is a common, essential, but sometimes unmentioned, feature of most analyses. Incidentally, it can also be an area analysts may be tempted to overlook, or to dismiss under the category of "analytic tact," because analysis of these issues may leave the patient hurt and angry before the benefit to him of increased realism is appreciated.

INFIDELITY RECONSIDERED

The persistence of human self-interest is of course closely related to intimacy and infidelity. For example, some of the chief matters that spouses tend, by and large out of courtesy, not to discuss with each other are their everyday selfish wishes: not to have to sweep the floor, take care of the kids, or take each other's needs into account; wishes to be taken care of without reciprocation; and certainly their wishes to sample different sexual partners. Does this withholding limit intimacy or permit it? Implicit here also is the matter of aggression. Communication to one's spouse of a fantasy of infidelity is more often an act of hostility than of intimate closeness. In considering instances of infidelity we must, of course, be alert not only to the opportunity of romance with the new partner but also to the anger of the betrayer to the betrayed. While this is often obvious, the shame- and guilt-inducing qualities of vengeful wishes can lead to powerful efforts to obscure them. In romantic love, too, the egocentric motive is often close at hand, to mention but one other example. The lover gives himself and his interests over to the beloved although the latter may at the same time be experienced as his own extension.

Now if we return to the case of Irv Schoenfeld, we note along with his neurotic conflicts, as part and parcel of them, a considerable amount of abiding neediness and self-interest. On the one hand, Schoenfeld renounced his own needs and wishes in order to take care of others. We are told that he cared for his wife and children better than he had ever seen anybody care for anyone else before, that he was a dutiful husband, that he took care of and supported his wife even when she seemed cold and aloof, that he had not masturbated as a teenager and felt prudish as an adult, and so on. On the other hand, we have the suggestion that he may have used his wife as a "way out" from his family—and later put his own interests first in a number of instances of infidelity. It seems reasonable to assume, in addition to the other dynamics that have been noted, that Schoenfeld was hurt and angry about the lack of gratification of his own ordinary, self-centered needs and wishes, both because of his need to renounce them as well as his wife's apparent tendency to withhold from him. There is an additional aspect: Schoenfeld evidently considers himself particularly good and moral. This suggests he may not have integrated negative and angry aspects of himself into his overall self representation. Having an idealized view of himself, he may thus have had less reason to limit his childhood omnipotence (Kramer 1995). Abiding self-centeredness and other preoedipal issues can make important contributions to understanding patients and their infidelities, even when the patient is rather healthy and neurotic. At the same time, the Oedipus complex itself, while object related, is also inherently egocentric since it derives from omnipotent childhood wishes.

REFERENCES

Akhtar, S. (1995). A third individuation: immigration, identity, and the psychoanalytic process. *Journal of the American Psychoanalytic Association* 43:1051–1084.

Appelbaum, A., and Diamond, D. (1993). The impact of gender on transference and countertransference. *Psychoanalytic Inquiry* 13:145–310.

Blos, P. (1967). The second individuation process of adolescence. *Psychoanalytic Study of the Child* 22:162–168. New York: International Universities Press.

Blum, E. J., and Blum, H. P. (1990). The development of autonomy and superego precursors. *International Journal of Psycho-Analysis* 71:585–595.

Brenner, C. (1973). *An Elementary Textbook of Psychoanalysis.* New York: International Universities Press.

Freud, S. (1923). The ego and the id. *Standard Edition* 19:12–66.

Gabbard, G. O. (1994). *Psychodynamic Psychiatry in Clinical Practice: The DMS IV Edition.* Washington, DC: American Psychiatric Press.

Kramer, S. (1995). Personal communication.

Mahler, M. S., Pine, F., and Bergman, A. (1975). *The Psychological Birth of the Human Infant.* New York: Basic Books.

Meissner, W. (1985). Theories of personality and psychopathology: classical psychoanalysis. In *Comprehensive Textbook of Psychiatry,* ed. H. I. Kaplan and B. J. Sadock. Baltimore: Williams and Wilkins.

Oldham, J. M. (1989). The third individuation: middle-aged children and their parents. In

The Middle Years: New Psychoanalytic Perspectives, ed. J. M. Oldham and R. S. Liebert. New Haven: Yale University Press.

Pulver, S. E. (1970). Narcissism: the term and the concept. *Journal of the American Psychoanalytic Association* 18:319–341.

Ross, J. M. (1992). *The Male Paradox.* New York: Simon and Schuster.

8

LOVE AND ITS DISCONTENTS
A Concluding Overview

Salman Akhtar, M.D.

It is only fitting to conclude this volume dealing with friendship, fidelity, impaired capacity for commitment, and extramarital liaisons with a chapter devoted to love and the various psychopathological syndromes involving it. Romantic love brings together friendship and erotic desire in a sustained, mutually gratifying, nonincestuous relationship between two adults (Freud 1912, Kernberg 1974a). Any discussion of intimacy and infidelity—two notions constituting the title of this book—would therefore remain incomplete without addressing the concept of love and the psychopathological syndromes of love life.

I will begin my elucidation of these matters with a brief summary of Freud's views on love. Then I will highlight the contemporary psychoanalytic contributions to this area. Following this, I will delineate five types of psychopathology involving love. The first three of these are relatively well recognized and include: (1) the inability to fall in love, (2) the inability to remain in love, and (3) the tendency to fall in love with "wrong" kinds of people. The other two are less well recognized, centering upon (4) the inability to fall out of love, and (5) the inability to feel loved. After commenting separately on each malady, I will offer some caveats to the proposed classification and thus render it clinically more realistic.

FREUD'S VIEWS ON LOVE

Seven years after having laid an intricate groundwork for understanding the nature of human sexuality (Freud 1905), Freud turned his attention to romantic love. In a seminal statement that still forms a cornerstone of the psychoanalytic understanding of love, Freud (1912) noted "two currents whose union is necessary to ensure a completely normal attitude in love. . . . These two may be distinguished as the *affectionate* and the *sensual* current" (p. 180, italics in the original). The affectionate current was ontogenetically the earlier one. It arose in connection with the early bodily and psychic care provided by the primary objects, especially the mother. The second, more specifically sexual, current came into being with puberty; it then had to be synthesized with the affectionate current. Romantic love could then be expressed toward nonfamilial objects with whom a sexual union was permissible and possible. At times, however, the two currents could not be brought together and this resulted in a psychopathological state. The sphere of love in such people remained bifurcated into tenderness and sexual passion: "Where they love they do not desire and where they desire they can not love" (Freud 1912, p. 183).

Freud went on to make distinctions in the erotic life of men and women. In men, there was a ubiquitous tendency for "overvaluation of the sexual object" (p. 181). Women, in contrast, continued to correlate sexuality with its earlier, childhood prohibition. To heighten sexual pleasure, therefore, men needed to debase their love objects (for example, to choose a woman who was socioculturally inferior to them); and women needed to mentally evoke (or actually create) the condition of prohibition.

Bemoaning the diminution of erotic pleasure in marriage,[1] Freud declared that "the psychical value of erotic needs is reduced as soon as their satisfaction becomes easy" (1912, p. 187). However, he added that there was perhaps something inherent in the nature of sexual desire that rendered its complete satisfaction elusive. The diphasic onset of sexual desire in human development led to adult object choices being mere substitutes for the original ones. This—coupled with the inoptimal expressibility, in adult sexuality, of sadistic and coprophiliac component instincts—made complete gratification difficult.

Two years after this contribution, Freud (1914) addressed the topic of love from a different perspective. He now distinguished between *narcissistic* (arising from the ego's self-affirming needs) and *anaclitic* (arising from the ego's desire for the object's help-giving qualities) forms of love. He emphasized that

> the highest phase of development of which object libido is capable is seen in the state of being in love, when the subject seems to give up his own personality in favour of an object cathexis. . . . A person who loves has, so to speak, forfeited a part of his narcissism, and it can only be replaced by his being loved. . . . Loving in itself, insofar as it involves longing and deprivation, lowers self-regard; whereas being loved, having one's love returned, and possessing the love object raises it once more. [1914, pp. 76, 98, 99]

---

1. While holding on to this idea in his later writings (e.g., 1931), Freud (1917, 1931) showed a greater optimism toward second marriages. Note, for instance, his statement that "(a)s a rule, second marriages turn out much better" (1931, p. 234).

Noting the interdependence of the two lovers, Freud hinted at the potential of mental pain inherent in romantic passion. He also noted the transcendent longing in love, since each lover comes closer to his or her own ego ideal through unification with the beloved.

In a subsequent paper, Freud (1915) noted that a synthesis of libidinal and aggressive aims was necessary for true, deep love. "Nature, by making use of this pair of opposites, continues to keep love ever vigilant and fresh, so as to guard against the hate which lurks behind it" (p. 299). He emphasized that transference love differs from normal love only in degree, and that "being in love in ordinary life, outside analysis, is also more similar to abnormal than to normal mental phenomena" (p. 168). This echoed his statement of a year earlier that love has "the power to remove repression and reinstate perversions" (1914, p. 100).

Still later, Freud (1921) elaborated upon the sexual overvaluation of the love object and traced such idealization to the love object's

> being treated in the same way as our own ego, so that when we are in love a considerable amount of narcissistic libido overflows onto the object. . . . We love it on account of the perfections which we have striven to reach for our own ego, and which we should now like to procure in this roundabout way as a means of satisfying our narcissism. . . . *The object has been placed in the place of the ego ideal.* [pp. 112, 113; italics in the original]

Then, in 1930, Freud again addressed the "unusual state" of being in love, stating that at the peak of such experience "the boundary between ego and object threatens to melt away" (p. 66). While acknowledging the exaltation that accompanies love, Freud once again emphasized the potential of pain in it: "We are never so defenseless as when we love"

(p. 82). He went on to note that many individuals protect themselves against the pain emanating from the loss of a love object by directing their love not to one person but to mankind in general and its cultural institutions. Such "aim-inhibited affection" (p. 102) constitutes the basis of friendship and familial ties as well.

In sum, Freud's view of love incorporates (1) its origin in the earliest mother–infant experience; (2) its narcissistic foundations; (3) the necessity for a fusion of affectionate and erotic aims; (4) the necessity for a synthesis of libidinal (affectionate and erotic) and aggressive aims; (5) a significant amount of renunciation of oedipal strivings; (6) the affirmation of ego ideal through the narcissistic strength drawn from the partner; and (7) an ego structure that can sustain a potential threat to its boundaries and the periodic emergence of the erotic scenarios dictated by various component instincts.

VIEWS OF CONTEMPORARY
PSYCHOANALYSTS

Later psychoanalytic contributors to the understanding of love followed divergent paths which, ironically, were along the two "currents" Freud had outlined as being intrinsic to romantic love. Some authors (such as Balint 1948, Guntrip 1969, and Winnicott 1963) focused their attention on tenderness, concern, and affection. Balint, for instance, noted that a special form of identification is needed for love, an identification through which the "interest, wishes, feelings, sensitivity, shortcomings of the partner attain—or are supposed to attain—about the same importance as our own" (1948, p. 115). Other investigators explored the erotic dimension of love, focusing their attention on inhibited (e.g., Bychowski 1963, Moore 1964), homosexual (e.g., Ovesey 1969, Socarides 1978), and perverse (e.g., Gillespie 1952, 1956, Ostow 1974,

Stoller 1975) forms of sexuality. Transcending this bifurcation, some later psychoanalysts indeed made significant contributions to the study of romantic love. Prominent among these are Altman (1977), Benedek (1977), Bergman (1971, 1980, 1982), Kernberg (1974a,b, 1991a,b, 1993, 1995), and Person (1988).

Bergman (1971) suggested that the bliss associated with falling in love involved a refinding of a lost ego state, namely that experienced during early mother–child symbiosis. Later (1980), he outlined five functions of the ego that are associated with this experience. First and foremost, the ego has to realistically assess the qualities of the love object and evaluate the future of a relationship with it. Too much reliance on reality can, however, spoil love. Second, the ego must integrate aspects of many childhood love objects into the love object of adult life. This task might be difficult if the early love objects were either at conflict themselves or simply too numerous. Bisexual identifications also need to be integrated and a mixture of the two components, corresponding and complementary to that in oneself, must be found in the partner. Third, the ego has to counteract the superego so that the love object does not become incestuous in the mind even though some similarity with the primary objects will be inevitable, even desirable. Fourth, the ego must counteract the inner pressure on "refinding the impossible, the replica of the longed-for symbiosis" (p. 69). Finally,

> [W]hen one is under the pressure of the repetition compulsion and the new object has the same pain-evoking qualities that characterized the old, every effort will be made to transform the new object to conform to the original object before disappointment took place. It becomes the fifth task of the ego to find other solutions. [p. 69]

Bergman emphasized that enduring love depends, to a large extent, upon "the transmutation of the idealization into gratitude for the refinding and for the healing of the earlier wounds" (1980, p. 74). He also declared that love's potential to give the adult what he or she had never received as a child imparts to love a great restitutional quality. Ultimately it is the harmonious coexistence of three elements that characterizes happy love relationships: (1) refinding of the early love object on many levels of development; (2) improvement on the old objects by receiving what one had not received during childhood; and (3) mirroring affirmation of the self.

The capacity to fall and remain in love also received attention from Kernberg (1974a,b, 1995). In his view, two developmental achievements are necessary for this capacity:

> [A] first stage, when the early capacity for sensuous stimulation of erogenous zones (particularly oral and skin eroticism) is integrated with the later capacity for establishing a total object relation; and a second stage, when full genital enjoyment incorporates earlier body-surface erotism into the context of a total object relation, including a complementary sexual identification. [1974a, p. 185]

The first stage is related to the integration of contradictory self and object representations, attainment of object constancy (Mahler et al. 1975), and of the capacity for in-depth relations with others. The second stage corresponds to a successful resolution of the oedipal conflicts. In a highly original statement, Kernberg (1995) pointed out a hitherto unrecognized aspect of being in love stating that

> it also represents a mourning process related to growing up and becoming independent, the experience of leaving behind the real objects of childhood. In this process of separation, there is also reconfirmation of the good relations with internalized objects of the past as the individual becomes confident of the capacity to give and receive love and sexual gratification

simultaneously—with a growth-promoting mutual reinforcement of both—in contrast to the conflict between love and sex in childhood. [1995, pp. 58, 59]

Kernberg also emphasized that it is important that higher forms of idealization persist within the loving couple. In his view, such idealization

represents the idealized identification, not with the body or even the person of the love object but with the values for which this person stands. Intellectual, aesthetic, cultural, and ethical values are included here; and I think this represents, in part, integration of the superego on a higher level, one linked to the new capacity for integrating tender and sexual feelings and to the definite overcoming of the oedipal conflict. At the same time, in this establishment of identifications with the love object involving value systems, a movement from the interrelation of the couple to a relationship with their culture and background is achieved, and past, present, and future are thereby linked in a new way. [1974a, p. 210]

Elaborating upon love relations in middle age, Kernberg (1974b) highlighted the vicissitudes of the reactivation of oedipal conflicts, at this time, in relationship to one's children. He also noted that the continuity between falling in love, remaining in love, and establishing a stable relationship does not guarantee a couple's staying together forever. The increasing capacity for empathy with another person, and the heightening awareness of one's own self that accompanies such a relationship might, paradoxically, lead to one's finding others who could serve as better partners. A deep commitment to one person and to the values and experiences of a sexual and intellectual life lived together usually prevents the couple's breakdown. Under such circumstances, renunciation of newer possibilities might even add depth to the couple's emotional and erotic life.

In a series of contributions spanning over two decades and culminating in a recent book (Kernberg 1995), Kernberg addressed the barriers to falling and remaining in love (1974a), the nature of mature love (1974b), aggression and love in the relationship of a couple (1991a), the nature of erotic desire (1991b), and the role of superego functions in the life of a couple (1993). Kernberg also discussed the impact of gender on the experience of mature sexual love. Citing Braunschweig and Fain's (1971) theories, he noted that, for both the boy and girl, early bodily care by the mother kindles the potential for sexual excitement. However, the mother's implicitly "teasing" erotic relationship to her boy remains a constant in male sexuality, whereas her subtle rejection of sexual excitement regarding her daughter inhibits the girl's awareness of her vaginal sexuality. As a result, men have greater difficulty in dealing with ambivalence toward women and need to synthesize the affectionate and the sexual imagos of women, whereas women are slower to integrate sexuality in the context of love. The way men and women handle discontinuities regarding love relations also differs.

> Women usually discontinue sexual relations with a man they no longer love and establish a radical discontinuity between an old love relationship and a new one. Men are usually able to maintain a sexual relationship with a woman even if their emotional commitment has been invested elsewhere, that is, they have a greater capacity for tolerating discontinuity between emotional and erotic investments and for a continuity of erotic investment in a woman, in reality and in fantasy, over many years, even in the absence of a real ongoing relationship with her. [Kernberg 1995, p. 84]

In keeping with the impressive breadth and depth of his contributions to the psychoanalytic study of love, it should not be surprising that it is Kernberg who has recently offered the most comprehensive contemporary definition of love. However, before quoting that definition, I will mention the contributions of Altman (1977), Benedek (1977), and Person (1988).

Altman (1977) highlighted the role of assimilated aggression and a benevolent superego in the experience of love. More importantly, he traced a "developmental line" (A. Freud 1963) of love. At the dawn of psychic life, a discernible self hardly exists and love is synonymous with primary narcissism. Gradually, through separation-individuation, libidinal investment of others—especially the mother—becomes possible. She becomes the primary love object. The phallic stage of development leaves a powerful imprint on love and when this imprint survives unalloyed in later life, in Altman's words:

> [M]uch of what masquerades under the guise of love is simply a compulsive effort to prove that one is the possessor of the penis, that one was never deprived of it, that one will some day obtain it, or that there is no danger attached to its employment. Satyriasis fulfills the need for reassurance of potency; nymphomania is the expression of a collector's avidity for the penis, albeit attached to a man. [p. 41]

The Oedipus complex, of course, introduces further specificity in the choice of love object, laying the groundwork for subsequent options in this regard. In latency and adolescence, altruistic and self-seeking components in love battle with each other. The characteristic drive upsurge in adolescence mobilizes both regressive conflicts of ambivalence and progressive trends toward inner disjunction from primary objects. Young adulthood permits the actualization of a sustained romantic tie to a nonincestuous object. Then marriage assigns new interpersonal tasks to love, the successful negotiation of which leads to a deepening commitment and gratitude in the couple. Middle and old age bring their own turbulence while offering new avenues for the expression of love.

> One recompense for the inevitable feeling of chagrin . . . that comes with advancing age resides in the relation grandparents have with their children. This love, like its predecessors, contains a narcissistic core. A grandchild embodies the grandparents' self-ideals and is loved as the grandparents would love themselves. [p. 40]

Altman also noted that women have a greater sense of commitment in love relations than do men. He traced this relative contentment to an earlier event in the girl's development, namely the shifting of her love from mother to father.

> This renunciation prepares her for renunciation in the future in a way the boy is unable to match. The steadfastness of commitment is, in this view, the renunciation of alternative possibilities, and the future woman has already made it in childhood. The boy has not, can not, and will not. [p. 48]

Benedek (1977) emphasized that the fundamental dynamic processes of love replicate those involved in a mother-child dyad. Through the repetition of mutually gratifying acts, each lover is internalized by his or her partner. Each becomes a part of the self system of the other. The demarcation between narcissistic and anaclitic love also diminishes within a couple over time. Marriage is sustained by the continuation of sexual love and the presence of mutual respect. Its permanence depends upon the ego organization of the two partners and upon their libidinal investment in the institution of marriage itself. Parenthood establishes a "biological link" (p. 75) between husband and wife and consolidates the psychological bond between them.

In a book replete with illustrations from history, literature, and movies, Person (1988) elaborated upon various aspects of falling and remaining in love. She noted that there are physical counterparts to the elation and the fear that accompany falling in love. She described falling in love as a complex affective state that included "agitation, a mixture of hope, anxiety, and excitement" (p. 38). Echoing Freud (1914, 1930), Person noted the potentiality of pain and torment in love. However, love also eradicates all uncertainties, dissolves sexual inhibitions, leads to a recovery of lost parts of the self, and gives purpose to living. She emphasized that brevity is an essential feature of passionate love. However, the capacity of the two partners for mature object relations helps them convert the flame of intense emotions into the steady glow of affectionate companionship.[2]

The relationship of the lovers to each other and, as a couple, to the larger group have also received Kernberg's attention (1991a,b, 1995). However, rather than summarizing his views in this regard, I will conclude this section by quoting his latest definition of mature love since it meaningfully synthesizes practically all the literature I have reviewed here. According to Kernberg (1995), love is

a complex emotional disposition that integrates (1) sexual excitement transformed into erotic desire for another person; (2) tenderness that derives from the integration of libidinally and aggressively invested self and object representations, with a predominance of love over aggression and tolerance of the normal ambivalence that characterizes all human relations; (3) an identification with the other that includes both a reciprocal genital identification and deep empathy with the other's

---

2. However, romantic love can only "survive and thrive if the partners are *cognizant* of difficulties as they arise, *communicate* their feelings to each other, and resolve their differences. There must be a real *commitment* to the relationship, which in turn will encourage the *compromises* that are needed" (Madow 1982, p. 135).

gender identity; (4) a mature form of idealization along with deep commitment to the other and to the relationship; and (5) the passionate character of the love relation in all three aspects: the sexual relationship, the object relationship, and the superego investment of the couple. [p. 32]

It is against the backdrop of such mature romantic love that the following five psychopathological syndromes of love life should be considered.

INABILITY TO FALL IN LOVE

Inability to fall in love is perhaps the most severe form of psychopathology involving love life (Kernberg 1974b). Individuals suffering from this malady have pronounced deficits in their capacities for concern, empathy, and basic trust. They cannot develop closeness with others. They lack spontaneity and manage their interpersonal lives on a factual basis. They also lack the capacity for "sexual overvaluation" (Freud 1921, p. 112) and idealization (Bergman 1980, Kernberg 1974a), which are mandatory initial ingredients of falling in love. Such people are too "realistic" in their estimation of others and cannot allow themselves the perceptual compromise needed for idealization of another individual.[3] An inward obliteration of gender markers, at times covered over by a patina of conventional gestures, also characterizes such individuals (Akhtar 1992a). Often they are celibate and given to masturbation with repetitive and banal fantasies. Even when they have somehow managed to enter into a marriage, they lack erotic desire and only go through the motions in their sexual life. Kernberg (1974b) also notes that, in certain nar-

---

3. Some capacity for idealization might be retained but is channeled away from human relationships into philosophical systems, politico-religious ideologies, or work-related realms.

cissistic men, the inability to fall in love is "hidden beneath an externally stable relationship with a woman" (p. 196).

Diagnostically, such psychopathology is associated with schizoid, paranoid, and severe sadomasochistic characters, as well as with malignantly narcissistic (Kernberg 1984) and disaffiliated antisocial personalities. Dynamically, the inability of such individuals to fall in love emanates from a "lack of activation of early eroticism" (Kernberg, quoted in Akhtar 1991, p. 751) coupled with impaired basic trust and poor capacity for sustained idealization of others. Attachment to others stirs up affects that are too intense for their deficit-riddled egos to manage. Loving is given up in order to avoid the dual terror of abandonment and engulfment (Burnham et al. 1969, Guntrip 1969, Lewin and Schulz 1992). Yet another difficulty arises from the unconscious envy that gets stirred up toward the potential love object because, if loved, he or she appears to be receiving the libidinal supplies that the subject desires himself. Not being able to fall in love under such circumstances acts as a defense against envy. The inability to fall in love therefore has both deficit- and conflict-related origins.

The developmental background of such individuals almost invariably reveals a history of severe, unmitigated childhood trauma. Physical and sexual abuse, parental desertion through divorce or death, and pronounced neglect of anaclitic and mirroring "ego needs" (Casement 1991) from the earliest years of life often form the background of this psychopathology.

Such individuals usually do not seek psychotherapeutic help at all. Instead, their ill-developed and frozen erotic life forces those around them into self-doubt, rage, depression, and, at times, desperate search for libidinal supplies. These significant others might appear at the professional's door, carrying a message of their partner's mute agony. Or the erotically dry individuals themselves might seek help, although not so much for their deficient sensuality but for vague persecutory anxieties and psychosomatic ills. In the treatment setting, a long drawn-out withdrawal that, in its most forgiving interpretation, can be seen as a "cocoon trans-ference" (Modell 1976), tends to ensue. The patient avoids all curiosity regarding the analyst, seems totally unaffected by the latter's comings and goings, and appears insistent upon doing analysis in an externalized, rational manner. In other words, the patient's characterological inability to fall in love becomes a major resistance against "transference love" (Freud 1915) in the course of treatment. Such development is usually indicative of an "ominous prognosis" (Kernberg 1974a, p. 191) for psychoanalytic treatment.

INABILITY TO REMAIN IN LOVE

The next step in the hierarchy of love-related psychopa-thology is the characterological incapacity to remain in love. Individuals with this pathology seem quite capable of falling in love and might do so over and over again! They retain the capacity for bonding, erotic desire, and idealization of a love object. However, after an initial period of infatuation, their love begins to pale. They start to be vaguely uncomfortable in the relationship, questioning whether they really belong there. Defensive attempts to ward off this disturbing senti-ment work only for a while. The dissatisfaction surfaces again although its sources remain unclear. In order to convert this inner distress into a tangible interpersonal strife, blemishes and deficiencies are found in the love object. A paranoid situation now results which, in a gesture of pseudo-magnanimity, is explained away as a "poor match" between the two partners. The relationship comes to an end, and after a brief period of emotional relief, the cycle repeats itself.

The dynamic factors underlying this phenomenology are complex and multileveled. Conflicts and deficits from various levels usually coexist, fueling and/or defending against each other in fluid dynamic patterns. Four nodal points in the hierarchy of conflicts contributing to this psychopathology are (1) a failed search for a "transformational object" (Bollas 1979); (2) anxieties regarding fusion with the object (Mahler et al. 1975, Mahler and Kaplan 1977); (3) mobilization of aggression when a primitively idealized object fails to live up to its promise (Kernberg 1974b); and (4) the object's gradual acquisition of incestuous qualities and hence the mobilization of oedipal guilt in the subject (Freud 1912). These dynamic patterns are not sharply demarcated from each other and have many overlaps. Yet it is useful to consider them separately so that the analyst's empathy is guided by a thorough knowledge of the psychological terrain as these difficulties enter the transference–countertransference axis.

The first dynamic pertains to the search for a "transformational object" (Bollas 1979) and a sense of failure in that search. A transformational object is the first object (usually the mother) and is "experientially identified by the infant with the process of the alteration of self experience" (p. 97). At this stage the mother is not yet recognized as having a separate existence but is felt as a process of transformation, and a trace of this feature persists in such object-seeking in adult life. Bollas emphasizes that

> in adult life, the quest is not to possess the object; it is sought in order to surrender to it as a process that alters the self, where the subject-as-supplicant now feels himself to be the recipient of enviro-somatic caring, identified with metamorphoses of the self . . . it is not an object relation that emerges from desire, but from a kind of proto-perceptual identification of the object with its active feature—the object as enviro-somatic trans-former of the subject—and manifests itself in the person's search for an object (a person, place, event, ideology) that promises to transform the self. [pp. 97–98]

Bollas goes on to emphasize that such anticipation of being transformed fills "the subject with a reverential attitude toward the object, so that, even as the transformation of the self will not take place on the scale it did during early life, the adult subject tends to nominate the object as sacred" (p. 99).

In the beginning of a love affair in which one is unconsciously seeking a transformational object, the object of his or her adoration appears to offer life-redeeming qualities. However, often that potential—even to the extent it actually did exist in the object—wears off. To begin with, the injured core of the self is seeking not only transformation but also revenge and is thus ambivalent and guilt-ridden (Akhtar 1992a).[4] Besides drawing structural benefit from the object, it also seeks to perpetuate the self-deprivation in an act of sadomasochistic triumph over the object. Moreover, in engaging the object successfully, the individual begins to be uneasy about having misrepresented his strengths and thus potentially oversold himself. Dread at being discovered begins to raise its head. Significantly, it is at the climax of the relationship that such individuals

> become fearful, doubt themselves, become depressive, and start to withdraw. Their conscious affect was one of anxious concern for the situation or the person in terms of either their personal unsuitability or unworthiness. They tried sincerely to disillusion others about themselves and sought by every means to be got rid of, rejected, and abandoned. One felt the plan had changed inside them. The movement was now in the other direction. . . . To leave the situations and objects caused them genuine pain, remorse, and guilt. They felt, however,

---

4. In a far-reaching critique of self psychology, Curtis (1983) has emphasized this very point: unmet needs during development do not result in psychic gaps or holes but in powerful affects, fantasies, and compensatory mental structures.

they had no option and so they became phobic and rejective towards the object. [Khan 1966, pp. 73, 74]

While aggression toward the object is here a result of self-defense, at other times such aggression is the primary source of the subject's inability to remain in love.

The second dynamic pertains to anxieties regarding fusion. Here intimacy threatens the boundaries of the self (Mahler et al. 1975, Mahler and Kaplan 1977), and being in love is experienced as a stressful situation (Gaoni 1985). A dread of surrender to "resourceless dependence" (Khan 1972) also lies at the core of this difficulty. The individual fears enslavement, even loss of identity, in intimacy and therefore withdraws from the relationship. However, aloneness also seems intolerable so that the object is re-sought in a fluctuating pattern of closeness and distance (Akhtar 1992b, Escoll 1992). At other times, one object is dropped in favor of another but the same conflict emerges sooner or later in that relationship as well. The descriptions of "ambitendency" (Mahler 1968), the "need–fear dilemma" (Burnham et al. 1969), and the "in and out programme" (Guntrip 1969) all speak to this very dynamic constellation, although from somewhat different theoretical perspectives.

The third dynamic contributing to the inability to remain in love has been described in detail by Kernberg (1984, 1995). It involves an orally incorporative and narcissistic cycle of idealization, acquisition, and devaluation. Here the individual does not have a true object relationship with the person he claims to love. Instead, he seems to be relating to an externalized version of his own grandiose self and/or a primitively idealized part object. Such an individual usually presents with a narcissistic character structure and may show a driven sort of sexual promiscuity. He might reveal, during analytic exploration, a desperate search for human love, as if it were magically bound with body surfaces—breasts or penises or buttocks or vaginas. The endless, repetitive longing for such body surfaces may emerge, upon analysis, as a regressive fixation to split-off erogenous zones caused by the incapacity to establish a total object relation or object constancy (Arlow et al. 1968), a regression caused by the incapacity to tolerate ambivalence, the integration of love and hatred for the same object (in the last resort, mother). [Kernberg 1974b, p. 188]

As the actual qualities of the hitherto dimly perceived object begin to force themselves upon awareness, disappoint-ment sets in. Aggression is mobilized and love evaporates. Unable to tolerate ambivalence, the individual now finds the previously idealized object to be "all bad." What was desper-ately sought is now vehemently rejected. The love affair breaks with much torment, at times, to both parties involved.

There is yet another source from which the inability to remain in love can arise. This involves oedipal issues. After all, the particular love object has often been sought owing to its "oedipally optimal" distance (Akhtar 1992b, p. 35) from the primary love objects. However, as the romantic relationship deepens, the love object might come to acquire a greater oedipal significance. In other words, each partner now more prominently comes to psychically represent for the other the desired but prohibited parent. Erotic union within them be-comes tantamount to incest.[5] Castration anxiety gets mobi-lized and defensive operations centering upon repression result in the conscious self experience becoming devoid of

---

5. Colarusso (1990) has recently highlighted how sexual relations in a married couple become oedipally recharged after childbirth. Ross (in this volume) also underscores the spoiling effect of the shadow of early parental imagos upon marital sexuality. However, long before such contemporary contributions, Horney (1928) had declared parental transferences in marriage to be the "funda-mental problem of monogamy" (p. 323).

erotic excitement. Love, which seems to have vanished from within the hitherto stable dyad (though most likely it has only gone underground), is now sought elsewhere.

FALLING IN LOVE WITH "WRONG" KINDS OF PEOPLE

Closely related to the foregoing dynamic is the tendency to fall in love with "wrong" kinds of people. Included among these are prohibited and unavailable others, such as those much older or younger than oneself, blood relatives, and individuals who are already married or are otherwise "unsuitable in reality" (Freud 1912, p. 18). All of these, in the unconscious, stand for the oedipal objects. From this equation, these objects draw their intense romantic appeal. Freud's paper, "A Special Type of Choice of Object Made by Men" (1910), eloquently describes the male version of this syndrome. According to him, the malady consists of two "necessary conditions for loving" (p. 166). The first of these conditions is existence of an injured third party. This requirement

> stipulates that the person in question shall never choose as his love object a woman who is disengaged—that is, an unmarried girl or an unattached married woman—but only one to whom another man can claim right of possession as her husband, fiance or friend. [Freud 1910, p. 166]

The second condition involves the existence of at least a "faint breath of scandal" (p. 166) about the woman's sexual behavior. The fidelity and reliability of such a woman is thus open to question. Indeed, she might be overtly promiscuous. Freud went on to state that men who make this sort of object choice display an extreme intensity in their longing and an unrelenting pattern of repeating the exact same scenario again and again in their lives. They feel a powerful urge to rescue the woman they love and feel convinced that she is in need of them.

Freud traced the origins of this syndrome to the "parental complex" (1910, p. 174) whereby the injured third party and the sexually tainted, unfaithful woman are none other than the father and the betraying mother of the night, respectively. Ten years later, Freud (1920) demonstrated the occurrence of similar object choice in a homosexual girl. A more common female version of such "special type of choice" (Freud 1910, p. 172) is evident in the "other woman" (Akhtar 1985)—a single woman who is romantically involved, either repeatedly or on a sustained basis, with a married man. Here the oedipal wish for the father is poignantly coupled with the hateful competitiveness with the mother and the guilty masochism at the attempted (and partially actualized!) overthrow of the oedipal boundaries.

To this now well-recognized, oedipal etiology of this syndrome, further impetus is occasionally given by preoedipal narcissistic and sadomasochistic trends. When this happens, the prohibited erotic longing acquires an even more pressured and despairing quality. In such cases, the chosen object not only meets the criteria outlined by Freud (1910) but is realistically almost impossible to achieve, inappropriate in more ways than one (for example, striking socioeconomic and intellectual difference), and/or more grossly "damaged"—to borrow a phrase from the novelist Josephine Hart (1991)—than merely having a sexually scandalous past. Many unhappy marriages owe their origin to a reckless enactment of rescue fantasies toward such a "debased" woman (Freud 1917). In effect then, while falling in love with "wrong" kinds of people is seen mostly in association with a "higher level" (Kernberg 1970) character organization, especially in the form of a hysterical personality, its more devastating versions are found in borderline, narcissistic, and infantile personalities.

In the clinical situation, therapists mostly see the relatively externalized portrayals of these difficulties through patients' endless talking about their rescue fantasies toward their love objects. In a married male patient, a frequent manifestation is an extramarital affair with the wife consciously or unconsciously cast in the role of "madonna" and the mistress in the role of "whore." Often the developmentally earlier preoedipal splitting of the maternal imago into "good" and "bad" part representations fuels and complicates the situation. In female patients, at times, the core internal scenario gets mobilized by the treatment situation itself giving rise to a powerful erotic attachment to the analyst. This, if preoedipal currents are received, can give rise to "malignant erotic transference" (Akhtar 1994), a matter closely related to the next psychopathological syndrome of love life.

INABILITY TO FALL OUT OF LOVE

At first, the suggestion that inability to fall out of love constitutes a psychopathological syndrome might appear strange. After all, is it not desirable for people to stay in love? A careful consideration, however, supports the validity of regarding as psychopathological a tenacious refusal to accept that one's love for someone is unreciprocated. Under normal circumstances

> if love is unrequited, it tends gradually to decrease and come to an end. On a deeper level, unrequited love activates the defenses against the oedipal situation and promotes the working through of mourning the unattainable object. As such, unrequited love has a growth potential—in both childhood and adult life. [Kernberg et al. 1989, p. 190]

However, in neurotic, borderline, and potentially psychotic characters, "love" tends to intensify when it is not reciprocated. This is because such love is actually a demand for preoedipal acceptance, for preferred status, and for omnipotent control over the love object. Through all this, and more, the individual is attempting to ward off intense aggression from within, stabilize a precarious instinctual economy, and maintain structural integrity of his or her psyche. Lacking object constancy, such individuals are excessively dependent upon external objects for the regulation of self-esteem and emotional well-being (Akhtar 1994). They cling to the defensively idealized object and often cannot tolerate frustration without regressing into murderous rage and/or suicidal despair. Individuals who remain tormented year after year by the memories of a failed romance suffer essentially from a similar difficulty.

Intense object addiction leading to pleading, coercion, and even stalking is another extreme behavioral manifestation of such impairment of object constancy. Its counterpart in the clinical situation is "malignant erotic transference" (Akhtar 1994) characterized by (1) coercive demands for "love" and, at times, for sexual gratification; (2) an unmistakably hostile and controlling flavor to these demands; (3) the absence of erotic counter-resonance in the therapist; and (4) the remarkable inconsolability of the patient. This syndrome, seen more frequently in women,[6] is most likely what Freud (1915) had in mind when he mentioned "women of elemental passionateness who tolerate no surrogates" and "children of nature who refuse to accept the psychical in place of the material" (pp.

---

6. The greater frequency of malignant erotic transference in women seems to have many explanations: (1) more intense reproaches in the female child toward the mother; (2) the extra burden on the female child's ego to mourn the "loss" of penis; and (3) the actual experience, in the background of many such patients, of having been "picked up" by their fathers after being "dropped" by their mothers. This last mentioned factor, while saving the child from a schizoid or suicidal breakdown, robs her of a fundamental prototype of mourning; instead, she learns that what is lost ("all good" mother) can indeed be found (an overindulgent father). The fact that such rescues are usually quite instinctualized contributes to sadomasochistic sexual fantasies and a perverse defiance of oedipal limits in later, adult life.

166–167). Important contributions to the understanding of this development in transference have also been made by Blum (1973), Eickhoff (1993), Joseph (1993), and Kernberg (1995).

The fact that such rigid inability (or refusal) to accept the reality is a powerful defense against rage becomes evident when the patient verbally or implicitly declares: "Love me or I will kill myself," or even "Love me or I will kill you." Here it becomes nakedly apparent that a combination of object coercion and primitive idealization is being employed as a last-ditch defense against profound, unneutralized aggression. It is as if the patient is saying: "Look, I'm carrying a time bomb in my belly and your love can act as a safety belt that will keep it defused." The problem is clearly inside the patient, not in the interpersonal situation.

INABILITY TO FEEL LOVED

There seems to be general agreement that the capacity to fall and remain in love evolves gradually and from many ontogenetic sources. Less recognized is the fact that to feel loved has its own psychostructural prerequisites. According to Moore and Fine (1990), "self constancy and sound secondary narcissism are necessary in order to feel loved" (p. 113). In fact, many other ego capacities need to be in place for this experience to occur. These include the capacities to (1) experience humility and gratitude; (2) recognize the value of the other, hence tolerate envy toward him or her; (3) renunciate a cynical world view and the masochistically tinged deprived-child representations of oneself associated with it; (4) relinquish infantile omnipotence and be satisfied with inner and outer life being "good enough" and therefore, by implication, imperfect; (5) psychically surrender to attachment, hence feel vulnerable to separation and loss; and, finally (6) experience guilt since some aggression toward the love object continues to emanate from within even under the best of circumstances. Many narcissistic, paranoid, and schizoid individuals lack these capacities and therefore cannot feel loved. In this context, the dark musings of Ben, the protagonist of Louis Begley's (1993) *The Man Who Was Late,* readily come to mind:

> Such as Veronique was, she made me happy as no one has except Rachel. Before she began to press me to act like a normal man, she made me a good deal happier. The poor dummy actually loved me. Rachel knew better: her idea was that, for a time, I could love her on a live-in basis. Probably that is all I am good for, although for a while, with Veronique, I made progress—I was beginning to be able to bear it, without wincing, when she was nice to me. [pp. 221–222]

To extend a popular psychoanalytic metaphor, individuals such as Ben do not lack mirrors but have impaired (or defensively compromised) visions! This prevents them from seeing their own (libidinally invested) reflections in others' loving and affirming behaviors toward them. They *are* loved but cannot (allow themselves to) *feel* loved.

A more problematic situation results when the inability to feel loved is accompanied by active attempts at rejecting, spoiling, and ruining the available libidinal supplies. This is most evident in individuals with "malignant narcissism" (Akhtar 1995, Kernberg 1984, Rosenfeld 1971). Such persons seek to destroy whatever love is offered to them in order to maintain a cold and contemptuous superiority over others. They mock loving and idealize hating. Consistently, they attempt to dehumanize, symbolically castrate, and destroy others. In becoming totally identified with the omnipotent destructive aspects of their selves and their internalized "bad" objects, they kill off their sane and loving self representations, which could develop attachment and dependence. The less disturbed among this group might rationalize their scornful

attitude toward love as a culturally superior form of emotional reticence. They are often wistfully aware of their inner
imprisonment but feel that there is little anybody (or they
themselves) can do to unhinge this Faustian bondage.

Clinically, the inability to feel loved is seen more often in
association with mild paranoid personalities. Here the deficient internalization of the comforting, constant mother is
associated with a lack of ego integration, untamed infantile
omnipotence, much sadomasochism, fragile self-esteem, and
intense separation anxiety. In this context, Blum's (1981)
concept of the "inconstant object" is highly pertinent. This
refers to an ambivalent loved object that is felt to be both
persecutory and needed. Such an object cannot be allowed to
have an independent existence. The threat of betrayal by it
must be tenaciously maintained. In a sense, this constant fear
of abandonment is the aggressive reciprocal of "libidinal object constancy" (Mahler et al. 1975) and a desperate effort to
preserve an illusory constant object while unremittingly
fearing betrayal and loss. In the clinical setting, all this trans-
lates into a rigid paranoid transference that secretly provides
structural stability to the patient.[7]

CONCLUDING REMARKS

In the clinical situation, each psychopathological syndrome
outlined above gives its own imprimatur to the evolving
transference. The inability to fall in love manifests as a sustained detachment from the analyst or as an "as-if" (Deutsch
1942) sort of compliance with the treatment. The inability to
remain in love leads to pronounced struggles around the
inherent ambivalence, resulting in marked fluctuations in the

---

7. In a related spirit, a character in Harold Pinter's *No Man's Land* (1975)
says: "I have never been loved. From this I derive my strength."

depth of attachment to the analyst or even a ruptured treatment. The tendency to fall in love with wrong kinds of people underlies the traditionally understood oedipal erotic transference. The inability to fall out of love is associated with the more desperate and hostile "malignant erotic transference" (Akhtar 1994). And the inability to feel loved emerges as a paranoid conviction of the analyst's lack of interest, if not dislike and hatred of the patient.

Such surgical separation of the phenomenological attributes and transference manifestations of the five syndromes is, however, ·more a matter of didactic necessity than an accurate reflection of clinical realities. In actuality, there is much overlap among these conditions. There is also a greater variability in their transference manifestations. Moreover, these five syndromes do not constitute an exhaustive list of psychopathological conditions involving love life. In focusing on phenomena encountered in psychotherapeutic and psychoanalytic practices, I have excluded the psychotic end of this spectrum. Prominent on this end are the "phantom lover syndrome" (Seeman 1978); erotomania proper (originally described by DeClerambault in 1942 and comprehensively reviewed in Segal 1989); and morbid jealousy of delusional proportions (see Mullen 1990 for a recent review of the pertinent literature).

Finally, while some of these syndromes (the first three, especially) do represent nodal points on a hierarchical continuum of psychopathology (Kernberg 1974a,b, 1995), the fact is that each of them contains deficits and conflicts from various developmental levels. The inability to fall in love, for instance, might represent the lack of activation of early psychophysical eroticism through a satisfying symbiotic experience, *and* a defense against unconscious envy of the love object, *and,* at times, even a pronounced inhibition resulting from intense castration anxiety. Similarly, the inability to remain in love might emanate from a futile search for a transformational object, anxieties regarding fusion with the love object, and/or conflicts related to narcissism, aggression, and the Oedipus complex. The implication of a developmental hierarchy in the various psychopathological entities outlined in this chapter should not, therefore, preclude attention to the multileveled nature of each syndrome itself. Keeping these caveats in mind, while being aware of the pertinent psychopathological terrain, will provide the analyst with the ego duality helpful in working with such patients. The analyst will possess both the inner resources for knowledgeable empathy and the capacity to be surprised by the patient's material.

Adding an element of surprise to this chapter itself, emphasizing the multifaceted nature of love and celebrating its lyrical quality, I conclude with a poem of mine entitled "Through You":

I have known love
I have known what it is
To be yielding while still in command
To be demanding and yet be kind
To be sensuous while remaining restrained
To be inviting but only between the lines
To be apart yet not distant
To be close without getting intertwined
To be concerned though not intrusive
To be respectful but not in awe
To be childlike but not childish
To be generous without emptying the heart
All this I have known through you
Through you, my dear
I have known love

REFERENCES

Akhtar, S. (1985). The other woman: phenomenological, psychodynamic and therapeutic considerations. In *Contemporary Marriage,* ed. D. Goldberg, pp. 215–240. Homeswood, IL: Dow Jones–Irwin.

_____ (1991). Panel report: sadomasochism in perversions. *Journal of the American Psychoanalytic Association* 39:741–755.

_____ (1992a). *Broken Structures: Severe Personality Disorders and Their Treatment*. Northvale, NJ: Jason Aronson.

_____ (1992b). Tethers, orbits and invisible fences: developmental, clinical, sociocultural and technical aspects of optimal distance. In *When the Body Speaks: Psychological Meanings in Kinetic Clues*, ed. S. Kramer and S. Akhtar, pp. 22–57. Northvale, NJ: Jason Aronson.

_____ (1994). Object constancy and adult psychopathology. *International Journal of Psycho-Analysis* 75:441–455.

_____ (1995). *Quest for Answers: A Primer for Understanding and Treating Severe Personality Disorders*. Northvale, NJ: Jason Aronson.

Altman, L. L. (1977). Some vicissitudes of love. *Journal of the American Psychoanalytic Association* 25:35–52.

Arlow, J. A., Freud, A., Lampl-de Groot, J., and Beres, D. (1968). Panel discussion. *International Journal of Psycho-Analysis* 49:506–512.

Balint, M. (1948). On genital love. In *Primary Love and Psychoanalytic Technique*, pp. 109–120. London: Tavistock, 1959.

Begley, L. (1993). *The Man Who Was Late*. New York: Knopf.

Benedek, T. (1977). Ambivalence, passion, and love. *Journal of the American Psychoanalytic Association* 25:53–79.

Bergman, M. S. (1971). Psychoanalytic observations on the capacity to love. In *Separation-Individuation: Essays in Honor of Margaret S. Mahler*, ed. J. McDevitt and C. Settlage, pp. 15–40. New York: International Universities Press.

_____ (1980). On the intrapsychic function of falling in love. *Psychoanalytic Quarterly* 49:56–77.

_____ (1982). Platonic love, transference, and love in real life. *Journal of the American Psychoanalytic Association* 30:87–111.

Blum, H. P. (1973). The concept of erotized transference. *Journal of the American Psychoanalytic Association* 21:61–76.

_____ (1981). Object inconstancy and paranoid conspiracy. *Journal of the American Psychoanalytic Association* 29:789–813.

Bollas, C. (1979). The transformational object. *International Journal of Psycho-Analysis* 60:97–107.

Braunschweig, D., and Fain, M. (1971). *Eros et Anteros*. Paris: Petit Bibliotheque Payot.

Burnham, D. L., Gladstone, A. E., and Gibson, R. W. (1969). *Schizophrenia and the Need-Fear Dilemma*. New York: International Universities Press.

Bychowski, G. (1963). Frigidity and object relationship. *International Journal of Psycho-Analysis* 44:57–62.

Casement, P. (1991). *Learning from the Patient*. New York: Guilford Press.

Colarusso, C. (1990). The third individuation: the effect of biological parenthood on separation-individuation processes in adulthood. *Psychoanalytic Study of the Child* 45:179–194. New Haven, CT: Yale University Press.

Curtis, H. C. (1983). Book review: "The Search for the Self: Selected Writings of Heinz Kohut," ed. P. H. Ornstein. *Journal of the American Psychoanalytic Association* 31:272–285.

De Clerambault, C. G. (1942). *Oeuvre Psychiatrique*. Paris: Presses Universitaires.

Deutsch, H. (1942). Some forms of emotional disturbance and their relationship to schizo-phrenia. *Psychoanalytic Quarterly* 11:301–321.

Eickhoff, F. W. (1993). A rereading of Freud's "Observations on Transference-Love." In *On Freud's "Observations on Transference-Love"*, ed. E. S. Person, A. Hagelin, and P. Fonagy, pp. 33–56. New Haven, CT: Yale University Press.

Escoll, P. (1992). Vicissitudes of optimal distance through the life cycle. In *When the Body Speaks: Psychological Meanings in Kinetic Clues*, ed. S. Kramer and S. Akhtar, pp. 59–87. Northvale, NJ: Jason Aronson.

Freud, A. (1963). The concept of developmental lines. *Psychoanalytic Study of the Child* 18:245–265. New York: International Universities Press.

Freud, S. (1905). Three essays on the theory of sexuality. *Standard Edition* 7:135–243.

_____ (1910). A special type of object choice made by men. *Standard Edition* 11:163–175.

_____ (1912). On the universal tendency to debasement in the sphere of love. *Standard Edition* 11:178–190.

_____ (1914). On narcissism. *Standard Edition* 14:69–102.

_____ (1915). Observations on transference-love. *Standard Edition* 12:158–171.

_____ (1917). The taboo of virginity. *Standard Edition* 11:191–208.

_____ (1920). The psychogenesis of a case of homosexuality in a woman. *Standard Edition* 18:145–172.

_____ (1921). Group psychology and the analysis of the ego. *Standard Edition* 18:69–143.

_____ (1930). Civilization and its discontents. *Standard Edition* 21:59–145.

_____ (1931). Female sexuality. *Standard Edition* 21:223–243.

Gaoni, B. (1985). Love as fierce as death. *Israel Journal of Psychiatry and Related Science* 22:89–93.

Gillespie, W. H. (1952). Notes on the analysis of sexual perversions. In *Life, Sex and Death: Selected Writings of William H. Gillespie*, ed. M. Sinason, pp. 70–80. London: Routledge, 1995.

_____ (1956). The general theory of sexual perversion. In *Life, Sex and Death: Selected Writings of William H. Gillespie*, ed. M. Sinason, pp. 81–92. London: Routledge, 1995.

Guntrip, H. (1969). *Schizoid Phenomena, Object Relations and the Self.* New York: International Universities Press.

Hart, J. (1991). *Damage.* New York: Knopf.

Horney, K. (1928). The problem of monogamous ideal. *International Journal of Psycho-Analysis* 9:318–331.

Joseph, B. (1993). On transference-love: some current observations. In *On Freud's "Observations on Transference-Love,"* ed. E. S. Person, A. Hagelin, and P. Fonagy, pp. 102–113. New Haven, CT: Yale University Press.

Kernberg, O. F. (1970). Psychoanalytic classification of character pathology. *Journal of the American Psychoanalytic Association* 18:800–822.

_____ (1974a). Barriers to falling and remaining in love. In *Object Relations Theory and Clinical Psychoanalysis*, pp. 215–239. New York: Jason Aronson.

_____ (1974b). Mature love: prerequisites and characteristics. In *Object Relations Theory and Clinical Psychoanalysis*, pp. 185–213. New York: Jason Aronson.

_____ (1984). *Severe Personality Disorders.* New Haven, CT: Yale University Press.

_____ (1991a). Aggression and love in the relationship of the couple. *Journal of the American Psychoanalytic Association* 39:486–511.

_____ (1991b). Sadomasochism, sexual excitement, and perversion. *Journal of the American Psychoanalytic Association* 39:333–362.

_____ (1993). The couple's constructive and destructive superego functions. *Journal of the American Psychoanalytic Association* 41:653–677.

_____ (1995). *Love Relations: Normality and Pathology.* New Haven, CT: Yale University Press.

Kernberg, O. F., Selzer, M. A., Koenigsberg, H. W., et al. (1989). *Psychodynamic Psychotherapy of Borderline Patients.* New York: Basic Books.

Khan, M. M. R. (1966). Role of phobic and counterphobic mechanisms and separation anxiety in schizoid character formation. In *The Privacy of the Self,* pp. 69–81. New York: International Universities Press, 1974.

_____ (1972). Dread of surrender to resourceless dependence in the analytic situation. In *The Privacy of the Self,* pp. 270–279. New York: International Universities Press, 1974.

Lewin, R. A., and Schulz, C. (1992). *Losing and Fusing: Borderline Transitional Object and Self Relations.* Northvale, NJ: Jason Aronson.

Madow, L. (1982). *Love: How to Understand and Enjoy It.* New York: Charles Scribner's Sons.

Mahler, M. S., and Furer, M. (1968). *On Human Symbiosis and the Vicissitudes of Individuation.* New York: International Universities Press.

Mahler, M. S., and Kaplan, L. (1977). Developmental aspects in the assessment of narcissistic and so-called borderline personalities. In *Borderline Personality Disorders,* ed. P. Hartocollis, pp. 71–86. New York: International Universities Press.

Mahler, M. S., Pine, F., and Bergman, A. (1975). *The Psychological Birth of the Human Infant.* New York: Basic Books.

Modell, A. (1976). The holding environment and the therapeutic action of psychoanalysis. *Journal of the American Psychoanalytic Association* 24:285–307.

Moore, B. E. (1964). Frigidity: a review of psychoanalytic literature. *Psychoanalytic Quarterly* 33:323–349.

Moore, B. E., and Fine, B. D. (1990). *Psychoanalytic Terms and Concepts.* New Haven, CT: Yale University Press.

Mullen, P. E. (1990). Morbid jealousy and the delusion of infidelity. In *Principles and Practice of Forensic Psychiatry,* ed. R. Bluglass and P. Bowden, pp. 823–834. London: Churchill Livingstone.

Ostow, M., ed. (1974). *Sexual Deviation: Psychoanalytic Insights.* New York: Quadrangle.

Ovesey, L. (1969). *Homosexuality and Pseudohomosexuality.* New York: Science House.

Person, E. (1988). *Dreams of Love and Fateful Encounters.* New York: W. W. Norton.

Pinter, H. (1975). *No Man's Land.* New York: Grove Press.

Rosenfeld, H. (1971). Theory of life and death instincts: aggressive aspects of narcissism. *International Journal of Psycho-Analysis* 45:332–337.

Seeman, D. (1978). Delusional loving. *Archives of General Psychiatry* 35:1265–1267.

Segal, J. H. (1989). Erotomania revisited: from Kraepelin to *DSM-III-R. The American Journal of Psychiatry* 146:1261–1266.

Socarides, C. W. (1978). *Homosexuality.* New York: Jason Aronson.

Stoller, R. J. (1975). *Perversion: The Erotic Form of Hatred.* New York: Pantheon Books.

Winnicott, D. W. (1960). Ego distortion in terms of true and false self. In *The Maturational Processes and the Facilitating Environment,* pp. 140–152. New York: International Universities Press.

———— (1963). The development of the capacity for concern. *Bulletin of the Menninger Clinic* 27:167–176.

Index